"All their Good Friends and Neighbours"

The story of a vanished hamlet in Angus

Catherine Rice

Number 55

Dundee

2014

ISBN 798-0-900019-54-8

Printed by Winter & Simpson, Dundee
(01382) 813813

to my husband

The author wishes to emphasise that the deserted hamlet
described in this booklet is located on private farmland.

Readers should be aware that visiting the site
may disturb farming and sporting activities.

Contents

List of Illustrations

Maps

Tables and Figures

Appendices

Acknowledgements

I could not have embarked on, or completed, this study without the help, support, interest and encouragement of many people in Dun, in particular the Rev Linda Broadley, Mr B. Aikin and Mr L. Mackie.

Mr Bruce Walker, Mr Duncan Macdonald of the Montrose Natural History Society, and his colleagues in the Montrose Basin Heritage Society, Mr David Orr, Mr David Walsh and Ms Alice Bremner all contributed local historical expertise and advice.

Ms Robyn Hukin, a direct descendent of one of the most prominent and interesting families in the hamlet, was of inestimable help in contributing family memories and photographs as well as genealogical advice.

I would also like to thank the following for their kindness in providing access to sources: Mr Ian Riches of the National Trust for Scotland, Mr Matthew Jarron of the Abertay Historical Society, Ms Kathryn Lamont of Maggie's, Mr Tam Burke of the Map Department of the National Library of Scotland, staff at the Local History Centre, Dundee Central Library, Montrose and Brechin Libraries, the Montrose Academy Librarian and pupils, and staff at Angus Archives, the House of Dun, the National Archives of Scotland and the National Library of Scotland.

I am grateful to The Strathmartine Trust and the Marc Fitch Fund for assistance with the publication of this work. Ms Rachel Benvie of Montrose Museum helped with funding applications.

Mrs Catherine Smith of the Abertay Historical Society edited the manuscript with painstaking thoroughness and sensitivity.

Finally, to Ms Elizabeth Sevo and to my friends and relations Roger Leitch, Esther Read, Charlotte MacDonald and Bob Rice who all read various drafts and contributed their corrections and advice: thank you for undertaking the thankless task so cheerfully and constructively.

Catherine Rice

Introduction

"a bright spot"

On the evening of Sunday 31 March 1901, a Highland tinker family camped beside the old drove road that overlooks Montrose Basin. John McPhee was a widower and was travelling with two young sons and his brother-in-law. John McPhee and his family, whose presence in this spot was recorded by the Census enumerator for the parish of Dun, may have been among the last travellers to pass by the then-deserted hamlet of Burnside of Dun, which for most of the previous century had been, as was recalled in 1930, a "bright spot" (*Montrose Review* 2 May 1930).

Villages have been abandoned since settlement began. Some have left no trace, not even a name, others still show their skeletal outlines in cropmarks, fragments of walls, corduroy patches of runrig. Two details distinguish Burnside of Dun: it was abandoned not during the age of agricultural improvement and amalgamation of farms, but very late in the 19th century, and it contains a small monument erected by two of its sons in 1930 in memory of their parents and grandparents "and all their good friends and neighbours in the vanished hamlet of Burnside".

I first came across Burnside of Dun in the 1970s, while living in Montrose. I began to investigate it then. I cannot remember now how I discovered it. Why I gave up the research is also now a mystery, but a few years ago I found the school jotter in which I had recorded my work and determined to return to it. The jotter contained, as well as copies of a few documents and texts, notes from interviews with retired farmers then living in Montrose who had played amongst the hamlet's ruins in the early decades of the 20th century. With the jotter as my guide, I started, more than thirty years later, to trawl through Old Parish Registers of baptisms, marriages and burials, Census enumeration books, estate papers for Dun and Craigo, the Kirk Session records, the parish school log book – all the usual 19th century sources for local history. In addition, I was very fortunate in being able to make use of a series of 19th-century letters telling the story of a weaving family in the hamlet and deposited in Montrose Museum by one of its descendents, Robyn Hukin, with whom I also had a very fruitful and encouraging correspondence. Although no-one alive today has a direct memory of the settlement as it was, I was also very fortunate in being able to meet and interview people living in the area today who know something about Burnside, who are interested in its history and who are keen to maintain its memory. These people are few however, and the site, now very overgrown, and its memorial have disappeared from all but the largest-scale Ordnance Survey maps.

Nevertheless, this hamlet is one vanished settlement that can be investigated and the lives of at least some of its inhabitants sketched out. This is thanks largely to the Victorians' meticulous efforts to pin down the lives of even the poorest inhabitants of these islands, by means of censuses, land evaluations and commissions of inquiry. In this case, inhabitants included agricultural labourers, linen handloom weavers, shoemakers and a grocer. Almost none of these people appears in the records of the large estates of the parish - not as tenant, subtenant or hired labourer. Some are recorded in the Kirk Session minutes, most often for their moral failings. The hamlet is not mentioned in the Old and New Statistical Accounts, written by the parish ministers. Even Violet Jacob, born and brought up in House of Dun and whose poems and short stories express her deep feelings for the ordinary people of the neighbourhood, has nothing to say in them or in her family history, *The Lairds of Dun*, about the ramshackle hamlet on the family estate. So this account also attempts, in E.P Thompson's phrase to "rescue … [them].. from the enormous condescension of posterity".

When I stumbled into Burnside in 1977, I wondered most of all about the reasons it was abandoned. This is still not entirely clear, and the evidence is circumstantial, but it is likely that a combination of a drift from the countryside and from agricultural jobs, the end of cattle droving and the condition of the houses were the main factors. The decline of handloom weaving was not a factor: handloom weaving in Burnside died long before the hamlet did, and handloom weavers were never the biggest group in the workforce, although a lingering story in the 20th century identified it as a weaving village.

My 21st century research raised other questions about how, why and when the hamlet grew up. These questions have been much more difficult to research but in my view more interesting.

The 20th century though, had the last word. Had it not been for the two men who erected the memorial and their love for their family and the poverty-stricken place which raised them, or for the owners of the greater part of the site who have left it largely untouched, both the attraction and the very name of Burnside might have completely vanished.

James C. Smith (1867–1947) was one of the men who put up the memorial within the ruined walls of his family's cottage. He studied at Edinburgh and Oxford, became a school teacher and rose to be the Chief Inspector of Schools for Scotland. He also published several books of literary criticism. In 1944, near the end of his life, he brought out a study of Wordsworth and in the last pages discusses the poem, *The Ruined Cottage*. Smith quotes these lines from the original version of the poem:

> Yet still
> She loved this wretched spot, nor would for worlds
> Have parted hence; and still that length of road,
> And this rude bench, one torturing hope endeared,
> Fast rooted at her heart: and here, my Friend,
> In sickness she remained; and here she died,
> Last human tenant of these ruined walls.

Chapter One

The hamlet in the landscape

"a number of small dwellings each having a small pendicle attached"

The remains of the hamlet of Burnside of Dun, an untidy rural settlement made up of a scattering of detached and connected cottages, lie buried in undergrowth not far from House of Dun. The hamlet straggled alongside the "cattle raik", an enclosed drove road, which used to lead from Montrose to the cattle market at Trinity Muir just outside Brechin. In *The Drove Roads of Scotland* Haldane explains that "where the land was considerably cultivated as in parts of Angus and Dumfriesshire ...attempts [were] made to define and restrict its route by the construction of 'raiks' as they were called, 50–100 feet wide with turf dykes on either side."[1] This drove road was one of many that brought huge herds of cattle from May to October, over one hundred strong, from the Grampians and the Eastern Highlands to the markets lying close to the Highland line such as Taranty (Trinity)Tryst at Brechin until the 1880s. On the other side of the cattle raik a cattle and horse fair was held twice every summer from the middle of the 17th century until 1891. In 1832 the fair was moved to the other side of Dun's Muir, less than a mile north[2]. The field opposite Burnside belonging to North Mains of Dun farm now bears the name Marketmuir and was the original site of the fair. The market was also a hiring fair for farm servants.

Drove roads in the Lowlands usually avoided main roads. Haldane (ibid.) recounts that stances, where herds and their drovers stopped overnight, needed payment in the Lowlands (in the Highlands they would spend the night in a suitable spot beside the road, without payment) and that "cottages or inns beside the stances offered, if they wished it, shelter for the drovers as well as grass for beasts"[3]. Burnside of Dun had a pub and a grocer throughout the 19th century and intermittently a shoemaker, who may also have made leather shoes for the cattle to protect their feet from stony surfaces.

John Thomson's 1832 map[4] shows a five-way crossroads at Burnside where minor roads or tracks from the Brechin to Montrose toll road met others crossing the Braes of Dun to Stracathro and Edzell to the North and the North Water Bridge on the North Esk to the east. North–south traffic criss-crossed the east–west journeyings of the drovers. Over the 19th and 20th centuries, successive maps show fewer and fewer "roads". The current Ordnance Survey map shows only the east–west cattle raik, now truncated a mile or so to the west, and a track leading south towards the parish church. These form two sides of the hamlet's triangular site.

In the 19th century, then, Burnside of Dun appears to have been well-placed to serve passing trade, and – as we shall see – to act as a kind of distribution point for migrating labourers and skilled workers, especially from the north. Its inhabitants did not have to travel far to reach larger towns and villages whether on foot or by train from Bridge of Dun station.

The third, southern, boundary is the burn that flows south from Dun's Dish, turns east and continues on into the woods of the Den of Dun. This rather insignificant and nameless burn fed the corn and threshing mills of Dun before disgorging into Montrose Basin.

This part of the county of Angus was described by Headrick in 1813 as "beautifully diversified by gentle eminences, fertile fields, plantations, villages, and gentlemen's seats."[5] In the parish of Dun, two of these seats were Langley Park, the newly remodelled mansion of James Cruickshank, a former Jamaica plantation owner, and the Erskine's House of Dun designed by William Adam in the 1730s, (and also benefitting from income from Jamaica). Both houses had large, beautifully landscaped policies. Four proprietors owned all the land of the parish for most of the 19th century. In 1822 when the first County Valuation Roll was drawn up the Erskines of Dun held most land, valued at £1582 1s 3d, with Carnegy of Craigo's Balwyllo estate worth only £700 in rents. Fifty years later, the total land holdings of the Erskines, including land outwith Dun, had been outstripped by those of their neighbours, Thomas Macpherson Grant of Craigo, and Sir James Campbell of Stracathro.

Together the four proprietors owned around seventeen farms. By the beginning of the 19th century, most of these were rented out to single tenant farmers, the old fermtouns having been amalgamated towards the end of the previous century. Improvement on the Erskine estate had begun in the 1770s when "improving tacks" were granted to some of the tenants of Leys of Dun and by the early 1800s most of the land had been enclosed, according to map evidence. The largest and wealthiest farms in the parish were Mains of Dun, owned by the Erskines, and Balwyllo and, according to the New Statistical Account (NSA) in 1833, had the very best land – "rich fields of black earth"[6] growing wheat, barley, peas, beans, potatoes and turnips. These crops would have required several teams of horses and armies of farm servants and seasonal labourers.

The Rev. John Eadie's account in the NSA goes on to describe the higher land – the Braes of Dun – as "flattened, wet and miry"[7]. The smaller farms of East Leys, North Mains and Damside were here, paying a fraction of the rent of Balwyllo and Mains of Dun. Burnside is on the boggy, marginal land surrounded by these farms. Between the drove road and Dun's Dish the land was mostly moor which, with its dense covering of furze and whins, would have been an essential source of building material and fuel for the cottagers. They probably dug up the turf too, when they could get away with it.

In this largely prosperous and prospering landscape, the hamlet of Burnside, with never more than 60 inhabitants, half hidden in a fold of the Braes of Dun, a scattering of clay and turf cottages on marshy ground near the burn, had an ambiguous and anomalous existence. Until it was abandoned at the beginning of the 20th century, there was no written account of Burnside. Neither the Old nor the New Statistical Account mentions it, both asserting that there was no village in the parish. Estate papers contain no records of a settlement. So its story can only be told thanks to the Victorians' concern to count, assess and analyse the population of the United Kingdom, especially the poor. Census Enumeration Books, registers of births, marriages and deaths and government inquiries into the poor law, the employment of agricultural workers, etc, have thus been the main sources in the chapters that follow. No oral memory survives. Even in 1977, when the present study began, no-one then alive remembered the hamlet when it was inhabited. Today, the very few people who even know its location know little more than what was published in local papers 60 or 80 years ago.

The origin of Burnside has proved the most intriguing but also the most impenetrable question, neither maps nor documents offering much help. The

Old Parochial Records (OPR) of baptisms, marriages and deaths in the parish of Dun record families living in "Burnside" from 1780; Roy's (1750s) and John Ainslie's (1794) maps show a couple of buildings in the area of Burnside – across the burn from Cotton of Balnillo.

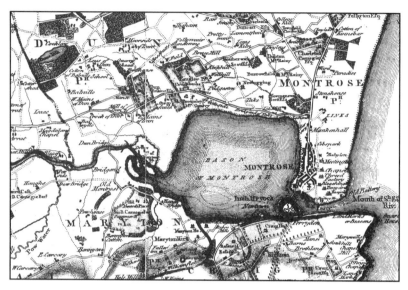

Map 1: John Ainslie, Map of Angus and North Fife (1794).
Map 1 Montrose. Detail. Courtesy of Caledonian Maps.

A *Sketch of Balnillo and part of Balwyllie* in the Carnegy of Craigo papers probably from 1800 (see below) shows no more than two buildings, one with a cleared area, likely to be a kailyard, attached to it, in the midst of wooded ground. It is not until the publication of the First edition of the Ordnance Survey (1857–1861) that there is detailed mapped evidence of a settlement although an estate plan of the Erskines of Dun dated 1850 shows the houses in the eastern part. The 25 inch to the mile OS map shows nine separate buildings, comprising up to eighteen individual dwellings. In the Ordnance Survey's Original Object Name Book for Dun, compiled to explicate the map, Burnside is described as "[a] number of small dwellings each having a small pendicle[8] attached, the property of W.H.K. Erskine Esqr of Dun". In fact the larger portion of the hamlet belonged at this period to Thomas

Macpherson Grant of Craigo. The 1861 Census lists eighteen households. The Second edition (survey date 1894) shows only four buildings, and six households were recorded in the 1891 Census. Eleven years later there were two buildings and by the 1928 Edition only one remained. This cottage still stands and is inhabited. It may well be the building shown in the 1800 sketch map.

Later in the 19th century, Burnside would probably have been known to many in North Angus because of its proximity to Dun's Dish, a favoured curling pond, described by the *Brechin Advertiser* in 1930 as "the Mecca of devotees of the roaring game, whose cries of 'Soup her up' penetrates [sic] the clear frosty air on a winter day." Dun's Dish was also the scene of a trial of an ice yacht in 1879 which attracted crowds[9].

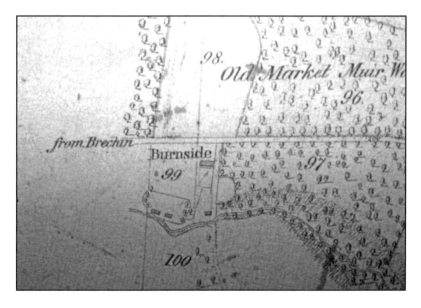

Map 2: Erskine of Dun Estate Plan (1850). Detail.
Courtesy of the National Trust for Scotland.

This attempt to tell the story of Burnside from the scant available documentary evidence has disclosed several large gaps. We do not know the economic relationship of the inhabitants to the landed proprietors and farmers – to whom did they pay rent, if indeed money rents were paid? Who employed them and how often? To what extent were they dependent on the produce of their kailyards? Were the weavers of Burnside self-employed or piece-workers paid by linen manufacturers in Brechin or Montrose? Who built the cottages whose remains can still be seen so clearly at the site? We do not know how the villagers fitted into the social landscape of Dun, dominated as it was by the Erskines, the Carnegys and the Minister – none of whom are recorded as having spared a thought for the huddle of buildings on the margins of their prosperous domains.

Towards the end of the 19th century, Fergus Friockheim Mackenzie contributed a series of "sketches" to the Dundee *People's Friend* describing the life and characters of an imaginary Angus village, the "Cruisie", based on his boyhood memories. His stories were collected in a single volume (which quickly went into a second and third edition) published in 1893. In the first chapter, he describes the village near the foot of the Grampians and half hidden in woods beside the River Noran. Although this is not Burnside of Dun, the topographical and social resemblances are close, so his account is worth presenting here with all its idyllic and nostalgic, not to say sentimental, touches:

> Many of the cottagers had an acre or two of ground attached to their cot, which they cultivated, and so eked out a moderate livelihood…Besides being farmers on a small scale, most of the people were weavers or found employment in the quarry … One or two lived wholly by the loom, and during harvest and seasons when there was a demand for labour, they lent a hand to their more fortunate neighbours …

> "In my mind's eye I see the Cruisie as it was when I was a boy … The brown thatched roofs mingled with the green leaves of the trees; low-browed windows studded with geraniums, overlooking the hedgerows which surrounded the gardens. Within those hedgerows, roses in full bloom were carefully trained up the front of the houses while here and there windows, small enough at the best, were lost in a wilderness of honeysuckle.[10]

NOTES

[1] A.R.B. Haldane, *The Drove Roads of Scotland*, 1952.

[2] Account of Dun, County of Forfar, New Statistical Account of Scotland (NSA), vol.11, 1833.

[3] A.R.B Haldane, p.37.

[4] J. Thomson, *Atlas of Scotland. Northern Part of Angus*, 1832. Available online at National Library of Scotland: http://maps.nls.uk/atlas/thomson/516.html.

[5] J. Headrick, *General View of the Agriculture of Angus or Forfarshire*, Edinburgh 1813, p. 5.

[6] Account of Dun, NSA, p.123.

[7] Ibid, p.124.

[8] Pendicles in Angus and Perthshire were rectangular plots of land varying in extent from 1 to 5 acres – "an adaptation of the long narrow fields or rigs that were associated with medieval royal burghs and seventeenth century burghs of barony" (D G Lockhart, Lotted lands in NE Scotland since 1850, *Journal of Scottish Historical Studies*, Vol. 25, 2005, pp 119-39). They were usually found on the outskirts of towns such as Alyth in Perthshire and feued to tradesmen. It is not clear if the Burnside gardens were actually pendicles.

[9] I am indebted to Duncan Macdonald for this fascinating detail, from a report in *Marine Engineer and Naval Architect*, 1 May 1879 available on openlibrary.org: http://www.archive.org/stream/marineengineera06unkngoog#page/n28/mode/2up.

[10] F.F. Mackenzie, *Cruisie Sketches: studies of life in a Forfarshire village*, 3rd edition, Aberdeen, 1894, p.5.

Chapter Two

Origins

"a most convenient place of the shire"

Markets and fairs were the high days and holidays of the country year. As well as farmers, cattle drovers and dealers, pedlars, showmen, hucksters, alewives and pickpockets would be drawn by the opportunity to separate country people from their hard-earned cash. The great Taranty Tryst was held on the edge of Brechin most months, but in May and June the only fair in the north of Angus was on Dun's Muir.

The author of *Cruisie Sketches* describes his fictional "Muir Market" of the 1840s:

> There was an abundance of fun and excitement at the Muir Market and towards evening the toll road…presented the appearance of a long and miscellaneous procession of horses, cows and tipsy people…the high turf wall was covered with weavers, quarriers and urchins who squatted among the broom and made jocular remarks to passing acquaintants.[1]

There was opportunity, or the dream of one too:

> It was wonderful the amount of dissatisfaction the weavers and the crofters of the Cruisie had with their existing stock as the market-day drew near. There were cows in the Cruisie which were as regularly taken to the Muir as the market-day came round because their owners "couldna put up any langer wi' them" but which were as regularly brought home again, their owners invariably going away sober, invariably returning otherwise.

The Act for a yearly fair at Dun, enacted by the Scottish Parliament on 23 December 1669, states:

> The king's majesty and estates of parliament, taking into consideration that the lands of Dun, within the sheriffdom

of Forfar, pertaining heritably to David Erskine of Dun, lie in a most convenient place of the shire where yearly fairs may be kept for the ease and benefit of his majesty's lieges dwelling near these bounds, for buying and selling of all sort of commodities, and whereunto all persons travelling from the north to the south of Scotland may have their bestial and other commodities sold; therefore, the king's majesty, with advice and consent of his estates of parliament, do hereby give and grant to the said David Erskine of Dun, his heirs and successors, a free yearly fair to be held and kept upon the muir of Dun, the second Wednesday after Whitsunday [*May/ June*] yearly, for buying and selling of horse, nolt, sheep, meal, malt and all sorts of grain, cloth, linen and woollen, and all sorts of merchant commodities; with power to the said David Erskine and his foresaids, or such as they shall appoint, to collect, intromit with, uplift and receive the tolls, customs and duties belonging to the said yearly fair, and to enjoy all other freedoms, privileges, liberties and immunities, likewise and as freely as any other in the like case has done or may do in time coming[2].

Dun's Muir Tryst, until 1832 just across the drove road from Burnside, places our settlement at a vital spot for the economy of the whole county. For the Erskines, the fair would have provided a regular income. When, in 1850, the Laird of Dun was obliged by debt to sell a sizeable portion of his estate including the land on which Dun's Muir market was held to Macpherson Grant of Craigo, the market itself and its tolls, customs and duties were kept in Erskine hands. The market continued until 1891.

Burnside straddled the two estates of Balwyllo-Balnillo (the western part) and Dun (the eastern part), with the former owning the slightly greater part. The Erskines of Dun had owned most of the parish until the late 17th century. In fact Dun was "once counted as 'one of the three great Baronys of Angus' which were ranked thus (forte metri gratia) Dun, Duddop (Dudhope) and Panmore (Panmure)"[3]. Over the next 200 years, their estate shrank largely due to the selling off of land to pay debts, while the holdings of the Carnegys of Craigo in the parish expanded. The farm of Balwyllo was part of Craigo until it was sold to the sitting tenant in the 1920s. When the National Trust for Scotland took over the Dun estate in the 1980s, the farm of Leys of Dun was sold and now includes the eastern portion of the site. The divided ownership of the hamlet is reflected in the names it is given in official documents. While the Ordnance Survey map sticks firmly to Burnside in all its editions, as do Ainslie, Thomson and Bartholomew, the Census enumerator names the place as Burnside in 1841, but uses both Burnside of Dun and Burnside of Balnillo (or Balneilo) in subsequent censuses.

The shrinking of the Erskine estate began in 1685 when James Mill or Miln, merchant and one time Provost of Montrose bought "all and haill the lands of Balwyllo and all and haill the lands of Balneilly" from the Erskines, anticipating perhaps the 18th-century fashion for urban merchants to acquire landed property and also suggesting that it was a valuable property.

James Mill's son sold the farms of Whitefield, Cocklaw and Leys of Dun back to Lord Erskine in 1722 and his grandson sold the remainder of the estate to Carnegy of Craigo in 1745. Balwyllo and Balnillo remained part of the Craigo estate for the next 180 years or so. According to the 19th-century Valuation Rolls, Balwyllo and Balnillo was one of the richest farms in the parish, second only in value to Mains of Dun which was on Erskine land.

Before 1780, according to the Dun Old Parish Register (OPR), no-one lived, or rather no-one was baptised, married or buried, from a place called Burnside in the Parish of Dun. Thereafter Burn-side of Leys appears twice in the OPR in the 1780s, Burnside of Balnillo in the 1790s, Burnside of Dun occasionally, Burnside in the 1820s and 1830s and The Burnside in the 1840s. These names are also found in the Statutory Registers of Births, Marriages and Deaths from 1855. However, on the ground, bounded by the drove track, the burn and the kirk loan, the triangular site looks like a single settlement.

Burnside may have been the successor to earlier settlements nearby. Roy's map of 1750 shows three distinct settlements in the parish of Dun north west of the House of Dun. Balnillo and Leys of Dun were fermtouns and the third was Cottertown of Balnillo. The Ainslie map of 1794 shows Cotton of Balnillo and, nearby, Leys of Dun both as scattered settlements on the other side of the burn. Leys of Dun had a smith – James Mitchel until 1790, then John Young – and many tenants and subtenants. However, this map shows only a single L-shaped building in the later site of Burnside, and two buildings on the other side of the kirk path (now woodland).

Estate papers tell the story of the improvement of Leys of Dun and its gradual transformation from a fermtoun with multiple tenants to two single holdings over 80 years. A rental dated 1720, shortly before the land was sold by James Miln to Lord Erskine of Dun, lists 25 tenants, each farming a tiny patch of two, three or four acres. By 1783 there were only six tenants. Holdings at that time were sixteen acres in extent each with a money rent of £8 per annum, so considerable amalgamation had already taken place. The new 1783 tacks (leases) state the farm is "presently possesst Runrig by" the tenant and others but are "now to be possessed distinct and apart"[4]. The tacks also lay down cropping rotations. It seems that older former tenants were not evicted as the new tacks specifically exclude their houses. In 1801, there were four holdings of equal size and the tacks make it clear that the tenants are responsible for the upkeep of "houses beyond the Burn" and are to agree "not to remove the tenants from the occupation of the houses on the other side of the Burn nor to raise their rents during their lifetime."[5] The people who lived in the houses beyond the burn were presumably former tenants of Leys, as one tack goes on to declare "…and the said David Thomson [William Walker, Elizabeth Baillie and Alexander Japp in the other tacks] agrees not to remove the tenants from the occupation of the houses on the other side of the Burn nor to raise their rents during their lifetime." We find David Thomson again in the 1841 Census, aged 70, living in Burnside as a farmer.

On the neighbouring Balwyllo estate owned by the Carnegys of Craigo, improvement seems to have begun with the tenancy of David Scott in 1780. The proprietor paid the handsome sum of £100 for a new steading for him, and provided lime, as a fertiliser, annually. Further enclosing and amalgamating of farms on this estate may have begun in earnest in the very early 1800s: a note from a surveyor dated 1811 suggests this, as does the sketchmap already mentioned.[6] From the 1760s (at least) until the 1790s, when the name disappears from the OPR, there is a settlement called Cottartown or Cottown of Balnillie. On Ainslie's 1794 map this is shown as close to the site of Burnside, although located to the west and south of the burn. This is the place where David Milne the shoemaker and his wife Jean produced ten children between 1765 and 1782 and where fourteen people died in the twenty years between 1777 and 1797. Balnillie (or Balnillo) would appear to have been a fermtoun in the 18th century (deduced from the mention of subtenants in the OPR) but also included a wright, a smith and two weavers.

An examination of the family names recorded in the OPR yields the information that three individuals who were born in Balnillo or Cottertown (or Cotton) of Balnillo in the 18th century were living in Burnside in the 19th century. We suggest that as the old settlements of Leys of Dun, Balnillo and Cottertown of Balnillo were abandoned towards the end of the 18th century and the land re-organised into larger farms, houses were built on the new site of Burnside, either by the landowners or by the cottars themselves[7]. In return for a stance for their house, possibly cupples for the roof and a plot of land for the kailyard, the cottars would provide occasional day labour. They might also have been given a couple of rigs in the arable land for potatoes or flax and the right to graze a cow. This was the situation in much of the Eastern Lowlands in the early decades of the 19th century[8] and was a common strategy of arable farmers and improving landlords. They needed to attract families who would be available for work during the harvest and at other busy times, but who would also have a trade and some land to maintain themselves the rest of the year.

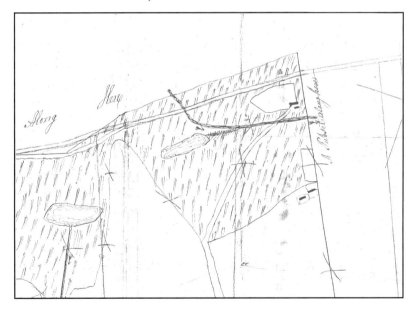

Map 3: Sketch of Balnillo and part of Balwyllo (c. 1800). Detail.
Courtesy of the National Library of Scotland.

The "houses beyond the burn" mentioned in the 1801 Leys tacks were inhabited at that time, as we have seen, by elderly former tenants. We may speculate that these were the first Burnsiders, and that when they died their houses (possibly houses I, J and K) were sublet to incomers. Frustratingly, however, there is no documentary evidence of such subletting.

Notes appended to the Census summaries of 1821 and 1831 mention the demolition of cottar houses in the parish, which had caused falls in population. Where these houses were is not mentioned. The Rev. John Eadie's testimony to the Poor Relief Inquiry of the early 1840s also mentions more pulling down of such houses in the parish as having taken place within the previous 5 years[9].

One other possible clue to the question of the location of Burnside may be Dun's Dish, the shallow lake about half a mile to the north. Dun's Dish may or may not be a natural landscape feature. It is not shown on Roy's map of 1745 and is not mentioned in the Old Statistical Account for the parish of Dun (1792). It does however appear on John Ainslie's "Map of the County of Forfar or Shire of Angus" published in 1794[10] and is described in John Eadie's report in the New Statistical Account of 1839 as "a lake covering about 40 acres of land, collected from the adjoining fields and springs for the use of mills"[11]. This may refer simply to Dun Mill comprising a cornmill and a threshing mill on the main road. There is a further mention of these mills in "The History of Montrose Water Works"[12] which, in telling the story of the search for new supplies of water for the town in 1852 mentions that although the Dish "was looked upon as a more substantial supply, its distance from Montrose was considered an objection, and the water in it was then used for driving several mills, for which compensation would be required". A recent archaeological survey asserts that Dun's Dish was "artificially created more than a century ago"[13].

It is conceivable that when the Dish was created or perhaps enlarged by drainage, the course of the burn was altered. Roy shows the burn as following a NW–SE course roughly in a straight line while in Ainslie and the OS First edition 25 inch maps it follows a north–south field boundary before making a sharp turn to the east to flow along the southern edge of the hamlet and into the Den of Dun. The burn then flows quite rapidly down the Den towards the Mill of Dun. However, the 1800 (or thereabouts) sketch map of Balwyllo and Balnillo in the Carnegy of Craigo papers (Map 3) shows marshy ground near the burn and three ponds, each with a rivulet flowing from it.

If the course of the burn was changed, and this marshy ground drained, a long narrow triangle of land between it and the drove road would have been created, too awkward a shape for a field and perhaps more apt to be the site of a new settlement. To this day, the centre of the settlement is water-logged and covered in a dense jungle of willows. The OS First edition 25 inch map also shows many wells near the houses, indicating a high water-table.

Until the 20th century the land to the north of the hamlet, between the cattle raik and Dun's Dish, was mostly moorland. This area is the highest in the parish. The two locations of the market would have been sited on untilled land. Thus Burnside was located on the very edge of the arable part of the parish.

The cottar houses of Burnside were probably not built by the proprietors or the farmers, as was the case of the well-known planned villages of Letham or Laurencekirk. More than likely they were erected by the inhabitants themselves, which would explain the apparently haphazard positions of most of them within the hamlet site. A plan of Balwyllo by William Blackadder dated 1834[14] shows houses B, E and G in the core area, as well as the outlying houses H and F (see Map 4 on page 60). The latter, together with A, may have been much older as they seem to be shown on the 18th-century maps.

What then would have been the attraction of Burnside to incoming families? One explanation may lie in the rapidly declining fortunes of handloom weavers at the end of the Napoleonic Wars: the chance of a cheap house in the countryside might have drawn weavers whose wages and standard of living were falling as well as the migrant population of agricultural labourers. In the 1851 Census, the first to include parish of birth, only two adult inhabitants of Burnside were born in Dun. Of the linen handloom weavers, five came from Montrose or Brechin and four from neighbouring parishes. Four of the agricultural labourers had moved from Logie Pert, the neighbouring parish to the north east, and the others from further afield – Aberlemno and Guthrie in Angus, Glenbervie in Kincardineshire and Crathie and Birse in Aberdeenshire.

According to the census evidence, the population of Burnside peaked at 60 in 1841. Twenty households are shown: nine of the heads of these households were agricultural labourers, seven were linen handloom weavers, there was a grocer and a journeyman wright, and a farmer (David Thomson, aged 70 and possibly retired).

By 1851 the population had fallen to 43. There were four weaving households and seven were headed by agricultural labourers. The grocer had become a carrier and a new grocer from Birse in Aberdeenshire described himself as a day labourer too. There was now a shoemaker, another Birse man.

The 1861 Census gives the population as 56, with thirteen households in Burnside of Balnillo and five in Burnside of Dun. Four of the heads of households were weavers, all now elderly, and another ten were agricultural labourers. There was another new grocer, this time from Inverkeillor. The cattle raik brought migrant workers and travellers as well as the drovers, and this would have helped to keep the grocer's shop going. Jane Anne Duthie, who lived nearby, in an article published in 1912 about her memories of the hamlet some 30 or 40 years earlier, wrote of "the shoppie, whilk did a fair trade till sae mony vans begond to rin the road"[15]. The "shoppie" survived until the 1890s. The grocer's residence moved from the Dun to the Balnillo part between 1851 and 1861 and the shop probably took up part of one of the rooms of the house, as could still be found in country districts in the 20th century. It would have been a general store selling basic necessaries such as cutlery, pins and needles, buttons, wool for darning socks, leather gloves for hedging and ditching, perhaps even boots and shoes as well as groceries. The first 80 years of the 19th century were the "golden age" of the village shop[16], as cheaper mass produced foodstuffs became more available and it was more convenient to shop locally than set off for the market in Brechin or Montrose, or wait for the pedlar. Keeping the shop may have been a part-time occupation for the shopkeeper: James Harper was listed as grocer and agricultural labourer in 1851 and although in subsequent censuses the grocer is given only one occupation, this may still have been largely part-time. The shop probably served a broad swathe of the surrounding district – the northern part of the parish and possibly part of Stracathro. The other grocers in the parish, according to the 1861 census, were at Bridge of Dun and Dun's Mill, on the toll road. There would have been passing trade too – drovers, travellers avoiding the toll road or going towards Stracathro and Logie Pert. The Erskines of Dun shopped in Montrose when in residence, and the larger farmers probably did so too – it was a few minutes away by train from Bridge of Dun station; but smaller farmers as well as farm workers would have used the Burnside shop at least some of the time.

Other reminiscences also mention "a rather humble hotel – just a cottar house – but it served the purpose of a place of refreshment for travellers by road, who were more numerous in those days than now"[17]. This establishment could not have survived solely on the droving traffic, which passed only during the summer months. No doubt other travellers called in, and locals frequented it too. Mr James Couper, a retired farmer whose family had farmed North Mains of Dun since 1874 recalled in 1977 that his father remembered seeing ploughmen passing through the woods on a Friday night, heading for the shebeen. It may be that the shop was also the shebeen.

The shoemaker who makes an appearance in the 1851 census, Hugh Ross, from Birse in Aberdeenshire, may have made and sold shoes in the hamlet, perhaps also shoes for the cattle passing on the drove road. On the other hand, there is a story that shoemakers lived in the hamlet and commuted every day to their shop in Montrose.

Handloom weaving of coarse linens such as those woven by Burnsiders was finally killed off by steam-powered mills in the 1860s, although fine linens continued to be worked by hand in Dunfermline and Kirriemuir. The 1871 census shows a small decline in total numbers, with only two elderly weavers and no other tradesmen. There is a new grocer this time with a large family including a grown-up daughter who is a dressmaker. In 1881 and 1891, well into the agricultural depression of the last quarter of the century, the population was falling rapidly, and very few of the inhabitants of the earlier censuses were still there. In 1891 eighteen people were living in Burnside in six households, only one of which had been there in 1881. The age profile had changed dramatically – one in three was over 50 while ten years earlier only one in eight was found in this age group.

The second edition of the Ordnance Survey map (an 1892 revision of the 1862 survey published in 1903) shows only the Beadle's house in the Dun portion and houses D, E and F as occupied in the Balwyllo/Balnillo part. House G is uninhabited and the ground between it and the burn is shown as waste land.

The 1901 census does not give the name Burnside to any of the houses, but some of the inhabitants of ten years before are still living there. There is no longer a grocer in the area.

The web of roads and tracks that spread out from Burnside seems key to both the rise and decline of the settlement. As the old maps show, especially Ainslie's 1794 map, other roads or tracks led north to Stracathro, Edzell and eventually the eastern Grampians, north-west to the North Water Bridge over the North Esk at Logie Pert (where there were extensive bleachfields and flax spinning mills) and thence to lowland Kincardineshire, as well as south towards Montrose Basin. An analysis of the parishes of origin of the inhabitants of Burnside in 1861 shows that, apart from the eighteen born in Dun, who were nearly all children, nine came from two parishes to the east, (Montrose and Craig), five from the south (the most southerly parish of origin being Carmyllie), three from Brechin to the west and as many as sixteen from the north. All these northern incomers came from parishes aligned along the two routes which led north: the Aberdeenshire parishes of Birse, Strathdon and Crathie were reached via Edzell and Fettercairn over the Mounth drove roads, and the Kincardineshire parishes of St Cyrus and Glenbervie by the North Water Bridge.

If the road system and its traffic help to explain the origin and evolution of Burnside, it may also explain its desertion. Droving declined rapidly in the later 19th century as did cattle markets. Dun's Muir Market ceased in 1891 although Taranty Tryst continued and still continues as a funfair today. But the shrinking of the agricultural labour force and the decay of the houses are, as we shall see, far stronger candidates.

NOTES

[1] Mackenzie, *op.cit*, pp.87-8.

[2] Records of the Parliament of Scotland to 1707, University of St Andrews. Available online at http://www.rps.ac.uk/trans/1669/10/133. Accessed 31/1/2012.

[3] V. Jacob, *The Lairds of Dun*, London 1931, p.11.

[4] GD123/269, National Archives of Scotland (NAS).

[5] NRAS 4346/9/2. Courtesy of the National Trust for Scotland (NTS).

[6] Carnegy of Craigo papers, NLS, Dep 267:74.

[7] The 1811 Census Enumerator (BM Add. MSS 6897) accounts for the increase in population of the parish since 1801 (from 651 to 680 people) by the erection of houses on Dun's Muir (to the east of Burnside) by John Erskine.

[8] M. Gray, Farm Workers in NE Scotland, in T. M. Devine (ed), *Farm Servants and Labour in Lowland Scotland 1770-1914*, Edinburgh 1984, p.11.

[9] Minutes of Evidences taken before the Poor Law Inquiry Commission for Scotland (1844), pp. 19-20. Available online from NLS.

[10]   J. Ainslie, *Map of the County of Forfar or Shire of Angus*, 1794. Available online from NLS http://maps.nls.uk/joins/577.html.

[11]   Account of Dun, NSA.

[12]   H. Hall, *The History of Montrose Water Works*, Montrose 1914, p. 94.

[13]   GUARD, *Project 795. House of Dun, Angus*, Glasgow 2005.

[14]   In private ownership.

[15]   J. A.Duthie, *Rhymes and Reminiscences*, Brechin 1912, p. 121.

[16]   J. Brown and S. Ward, *The Village Shop* Salisbury 1990, p.14.

[17]   Andrew Lamb, overseer on the Dun Estate, quoted in the *Montrose Review* 2 May 1930

Chapter Three

Inhabitants

"stout labourers"

In the 1841 Census, the first to supply people's names, there were 60 inhabitants living in twenty households in Burnside. Seventeen men and seven single women had occupations listed: it was the practice of 19th-century censuses to ignore the paid work of married women. Nine worked as agricultural labourers, ten as linen handloom weavers, there was one grocer and one wright, two female servants and a farmer.

Twenty years later, the total population and the demographic profile of the settlement had hardly altered at all. There were 56 inhabitants. The number of agricultural labourers had risen to fifteen, many of them seasonal migrants working as ditchers (most were boarders originating from Ireland). There were eight weavers, a grocer and a road labourer.

The last censuses of the 19th century saw the population fall rapidly, to 26 in 1881 and eighteen in 1891, reflecting both the national decline in the agricultural labour force and the increasing isolation, inconvenience and probably the discomfort of the hamlet and its houses. Even by 1871 there were no active tradesmen, all the employed adult males working as farm servants or labourers. However, there was still a shopkeeper ("merchant general") in 1891.

The proportion of older residents was significantly higher than the Eastern Lowlands of Scotland as a whole. At a time when life expectancy, even for one year-olds, was around 47, the proportion of elderly residents in Burnside was striking. The percentage of children was around the same as in the Eastern Lowlands, while the percentage of people of working age was often lower, as the figure overleaf shows.[1]

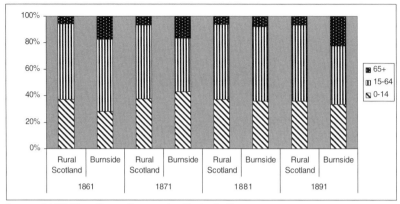

Sources: M W Flinn; Census Enumeration Books for Dun

Figure 3.1 Age structure of the Burnside population 1861–1891

The census data show several elderly couples and single people living on their own, and in 1871 four households which included both elderly grandparents and grandchildren, some illegitimate (see chapter 7).

Most rural dwellers in 19th century lowland Scotland were farm servants and their families, living on or around farms. Villages were rare – there were no villages in Dun or in its surrounding parishes of Maryton, Stracathro and Farnell. A hamlet such as Burnside may therefore have been a haven for people too old to work full time as servants while still able to take on part-time or lighter labouring work and to work their kailyards. The 1851 census seems anomalous with below average numbers of children and old people and a high proportion of people of working age: well over half the population was employed in that census. The total population also dipped. Although the OPR, as has been noted, is notoriously unreliable, the Dun record shows that the 1840s saw more than twice as many burials in Dun (twenty) as in the decades before and after (including deaths registered statutorily from 1855). It is tempting to conclude that the epidemic illnesses of the early and late 1840s were to blame. The OPR does not give causes of deaths but the epidemics which affected rural areas at this time were of typhus, the "poor man's disease", and scarlet fever, which mainly killed children[2]. As the 1840s was also a time of economic depression, poverty and undernourishment are likely to have been major factors contributing to the effect of such epidemic illnesses.

The relatively large number of children of school age and the very small number of people in their teens and early twenties says more about work patterns than about family size: after the age of twelve or thirteen, nearly all children would have left home to learn a trade or enter service on a farm. Marriage in rural areas was not common until the mid-twenties for women and later for men due largely to employment patterns (unmarried farm servants were often preferred) and a shortage of affordable housing.

	1841	1851	1861	1871	1881	1891
Eastern Lowlands	89.1	89.9	88.1	88.3	89.7	90.4
Burnside	53.1	72.0	78.1	63.3	78.6	100

Sources: M W Flinn; Census Enumeration Books for Dun

Table 3.1 Sex ratios, all age-groups in Eastern Lowland Scotland and in Burnside, 1841–91, expressed as the ratio of males to every 100 females

Table 3.1 shows the number of males for every 100 females. The huge gender gap in 1841 was largely due to the presence of 15 girls under the age of 14 compared with only three boys. A closer look at the census data for 1851 shows that it is males in their 50s who are missing. After that the 'lost' men are in their teens and twenties, the ages when they are most likely to have been living as servants on farms.

As has already been discussed, Burnside of Dun was most likely a successor to Cottartown of Balnillo and the fermtouns of Balnillo and Leys of Dun. OPR and census data tell us that at least six people who were born in these settlements in the 18th and early 19th century were living in Burnside in the 1830s and 1840s. They included David Thomson, "late farmer in the Leys of Dun" who was born in 1769, one of the large family of John Thomson, tenant in Leys, and who died in Burnside in 1847. Robert Miln and Robert Smith and their wives lived in Cottartown of Balnillo in the 18th century and ended their days in Burnside. John Young, blacksmith, was born in the Leys, son of the smith there, and was living in Burnside in 1839 when his third daughter was born.If the earlier inhabitants had moved only a short distance from the old cottartouns, probably after they were demolished, later arrivals came from further afield. From the 1851 Census, which for the first time collected data on parishes of birth, we learn that only two adults were born in Dun. One of these was Robert Smith's widow and the other his son James, whom we will meet later. Nearly all the other adult inhabitants had been born in Angus parishes. Ten years later, of the 43 inhabitants of working age, only six, including three in their teens, were born in Dun, 25 elsewhere in the county and twelve outwith Forfarshire, including five Irish labourers. This reinforces the view that the settlement attracted migrant workers and their families.

As well as changes in the patterns of origins and occupations of the inhabitants over the century, other demographic changes are revealed by the Censuses. Table 3.2 shows, amongst other aspects, the percentage of households that were still in Burnside after twenty years.

Census year	Population	M	F	No. of households	Average age	Average household size	% children aged 13 and under	Persistence over 2 censuses (i)
1841	60	21	39	17	35(ii)	3.5	28	n/a
1851	43	18	25	16	34	2.7	21	n/a
1861	56	24	32	18	35	3.1	29	29.4%
1871	49	19	30	11	29	4.5	43	18.8%
1881	25	11	14	8	28	3.1	36	11.1%
1891	18	9	9	6	36	3	33	n/a

Sources: Census Enumeration Books for Dun

(i) This column represents the percentage of households living in Burnside over a span of 3 censuses: 1841–1861, 1851–1871 and 1861–1881. No-one living there in 1891 had appeared in the 1871 census.

(ii) The 1841 Census recorded the ages of persons over 15 years of age to the nearest 5 years.

Table 3.2 Demographic change and stability over 50 years

Our perception today of rural life in the past is of stable, almost unchanging communities where trades and occupations were handed down from father to son and where no-one travelled far in their daily lives or moved house after marriage. The well-known exception to this were the farmservants who often changed jobs and homes every year. In Burnside, although there were no farmservants, over the latter half of the 19th century there was a 66% turnover in households each census, and this became much more marked towards the end of the century. The "stayers" included two families, the Cruikshanks and the Moirs, who remained in the hamlet for nearly 60 years. Alexander Steel and his wife Helen Symm or Simond appear in the four Censuses with various children and grandchildren from 1841 to 1871. The Penders lived at Burnside for at least 25 years as did Christina Smith and her daughters. No other families stayed so long.

The statutory registers of births, marriages and deaths, which begin in 1855, tell us of some of those who lived in Burnside for less than ten years. They were mostly agricultural labourers but there were also tradesmen such as Alexander Buick, a master shoemaker, Andrew Rodger, a blacksmith and George Cathro, a miller. The last named was living there in 1880.

Most adults, as we have seen, were not born in Dun, but had not moved far to get to Burnside. Amongst the birthplaces listed in the 1851 Census, five were in Aberdeenshire and one in Kincardineshire. But 21 inhabitants had been born in neighbouring parishes (Logie Pert, Brechin, Montrose, Farnell, Stracathro) and the rest in parishes only a little further away (Craig, Lethnot and Navar, Aberlemno, Guthrie, Carmyllie). From the midpoint of Dun parish to the midpoints of these parishes was less than 15 miles. Fifteen miles was reckoned to be a reasonable distance for anyone to walk in a day. Ingram quotes a reminiscence published in 1872: "twenty or 30 miles were thought nothing of, even for women to walk" at the beginning of the 19th century.

Jennifer Ingram's groundbreaking study of mobility in Angus in the first stage of the agricultural and industrial revolutions, 1780 to 1830[3], has shown that geographical mobility, both temporary and longer-term, was much more common in the countryside than was previously believed. Day labourers walking to and from a ditching or dyking job, families visiting towns and fairs for the day, urban or rural handloom weavers spending the summer months harvesting away from home, farm servants changing jobs every six or twelve months – such "circular mobility" brought rural communities in touch with each other and helped to restructure rural society.

One way of measuring longer-term mobility is to count the number of men and women who married spouses from other parishes. Ingram investigated this factor for 16 parishes in Angus, and shows that Dun in the 1790s had the highest rate of marrying outwith the parish ("exogamous marriage") in the sample. This could either be due to a shortage of partners in the parish or simply to higher than average mobility. On the other hand, the marriage records in the OPR include six marriages of Burnside inhabitants and all but one were endogamous (both partners were "of this parish"), between 1820 and 1848.

By 1851, not only were the majority of adults in Burnside incomers, but of the eight couples only one husband and wife were born in the same parish. It seems that mobility increased around the middle of the century. The children of the former small tenant farmers, the cottars and the weavers who moved to Burnside at the beginning of the 1800s did not remain there, and the houses were taken by incomers. But even in 1881, these incomers came on the whole from parishes in the north of the county: Marykirk, Farnell, Logie Pert, Menmuir and Stracathro. Only one adult in the 1881 Census was born in Dun. This was James Falconer, a retired joiner, returning to Burnside after nearly half a century. One family, the Wilkies, came from further afield in Fife.

Working life

For most of the 19th century, children who went to school were expected to attend from the age of five to thirteen years, but mainly during the winter months. Many children started work around the age of nine or ten, working as herds in the countryside. After twelve or thirteen, country children expected to leave home to find work, and to live with their employer. John Stool, the brother of the weaver Elizabeth Moir of Burnside, left home when he was twelve and worked for a relative, a carrier, in Montrose. At fourteen, he started to learn weaving with his father. In the 1830s, it was reckoned that handloom weavers needed no more than two or three years' training and could start to earn half wages after a few months, at the age of twelve or thirteen[4]. As we shall see, there were Burnside weavers in their teens.

For agricultural workers the mid-twenties was the usual time for marrying and finding their own home. So for twelve or thirteen years, young people of both sexes lived and worked on farms, often, in Angus, in bothies or chaumers with other unmarried workers. As we have seen, few children in Burnside over the age of thirteen still lived at home. In the later decades of the century compulsory education and the agricultural depression kept more older children at home. There was clearly a lot of to-ing and fro-ing, especially of daughters. At the age of fifteen in 1841, Isabella Moir, John Stool's niece, was living next door to her mother, employed as a female servant by another weaver. In the same year, Alexander Steel an agricultural labourer and his wife Helen were living with three daughters aged thirteen, seven and five. Ten years later, all these girls had left home and an older daughter, aged twenty-eight, had come back and was working as an agricultural labourer. Her sister Isabella, a linen bleacher who may have been employed at the bleachworks in Logie Pert, was at home in 1865 to give birth to an illegitimate son. In 1861 Thomas Pender and his wife Catherine were living with three children under seven in 1861; ten years later they had four children under ten and their thirteen-year-old daughter was a servant with an equally large neighbouring family – that of Joseph Smart.

The agricultural labourers of Burnside were hired by the day, as required. Outwith seed-time and harvest, they would tend their plots of land. They worked on the land until they fell ill or died. In 1841 there were three agricultural labourers over the age of 70. In later censuses, the elderly were more likely to be described as retired, but George Menmuir was still apparently working on the land in 1891 at the age of 71 before he was employed as the Church Beadle.

We do not know exactly who employed the agricultural labourers, but the large arable farms of Balwyllo and Balnillo, Mains of Dun and North Mains of Dun would have needed armies of workers, adults as well as children, from early spring to late autumn. All the work would have been casual, seasonal and poorly paid and there would have been long periods of unemployment or underemployment. The 1861 Census Enumeration Books tell us that Mains of Dun, where the farmer also ran a tileworks, employed nine ploughmen, nine labourers, three boys and seventeen women. Balwyllo employed thirteen men, two boys and five women. By contrast East and West Leys had only two men, four boys and a girl between them. The census enumeration books however, can on occasion conceal more than they reveal. Thomas Pender, an Irishman, who is described as an agricultural labourer in three censuses was also a drainage contractor. He appears in the Register of Improvements to entailed estates for Angus as contracting, along with his neighbour in Burnside, James Wallace, to cut drains on East and West Leys of Dun in 1860, and again in 1868. The men were paid £13 16s 6d in 1860 and £18 9s 0d in 1868. We can assume that the four Irish ditchers in the 1861 census who were lodging with Homer Cruikshank and James Broadley, a ditcher from Ireland who lodged with the Penders, were all engaged on this work.

Other sources of employment for labourers in the parish were the quarries (one in the Den of Dun nearby), the tileworks at Mains of Dun and at Pugeston, the toll road and the railway.

The depopulation of Burnside coincided with the agricultural recession of the late 19th century and the decline in the agricultural population. In Scotland between 1871 and 1901 around one third of the male farm servants and labourers left the land. The reasons are complex. Devine (1984) argues that social isolation, long working hours, rare holidays, poor housing and often miserable working conditions are more likely "push" factors than wages or mechanisation which may rather have been a consequence of this flight from the land[5]. Even more women abandoned farm work. Women were never paid more than half the wages of their male counterparts, although their work could be even harder. Agriculture was increasingly coming to be seen as "unwomanlike", especially in an age when jobs in domestic service, shops and offices were more available, cleaner and more attractive – and more in reach thanks to compulsory education and the railways.

Nevertheless, in 1881, Balwyllo was employing fourteen men, a boy and four women and Mains – no longer making tiles – still had fourteen men, seven women and two boys.

What kind of work did women farmworkers undertake? On the mixed farms of the area there would have been sowing of cereals, peas and beans in early spring, potato planting in late spring, turnip planting then hoeing through the summer followed by haymaking and the harvest, as well as work around the steading. Ann Simpson, a 30 year old agricultural labourer, was haymaking at Balwyllo when she committed the sin of antenuptial fornication (see chapter 7).

"Stout labourers" could earn 1s 6d or 1s 10d in the early 1830s, according to the Reverend John Eadie's account of Dun in the NSA. Women working outdoors were paid 8d – less than half the men's rate. Unlike the ploughmen, seen as the aristocrats of the farm workforce, day labourers were paid wholly in cash, and might have had to pay rent from their wages. Work must have been intermittent for much of the year so their plots of land would have been vital for their survival.

Sixty years later, men's wages had roughly doubled. There is no direct evidence from Dun, but farmers in the county told the Royal Commission on Labour in the mid-1890s that "orra [extra] labourers" were earning 3s a day, and women or lads 1s 4d or 1s 6d and more for planting potatoes, hoeing (mainly done by the latter) and during harvest.

At harvest time, which usually began in mid-August and might continue until late September, men, women and children, would pitch in. Farms in Dun employed threavers to bring in the harvest. Each threaver worked by him or herself, cutting along the ridge, and was paid by the number of threaves (a measure of cut grain containing two full stooks of 24 sheaves of oats or barley or 28 sheaves of wheat) cut each day. Harvesting was thus attractive to tradesmen and townspeople who could hire themselves out for a few days or as long as suited them: threavers were not hired for the whole harvest season as happened in more cereal-intensive regions. The use of the heavier, long-handled scythe for grain harvesting was taking over from the sickle or heuk from the beginning of the 19th century, starting in the northeast, and this excluded women, who had been preferred in the days of the sickle. Women were now mainly employed to gather sheaves and build the threaves.

School holidays were scheduled to allow the pupils to take part in the cereal harvest. The school was closed from the middle of August for around 6 weeks. It was not until 1891 that the start of the summer holiday was moved to the end of June and the return to school to the middle of August, as it is today. However, around one third of the children might be absent during potato planting time in April and for the tattie-howking in October–November. In fact, in 1879, the Dun School Board, made up of landowners and farmers, excused children from compulsory attendance for ten days in April "in order that, if required, they may assist in planting the Potatoe Crop".

NOTES

[1]   M.W. Flinn (ed), *Scottish Population History from the 17th century to the 1930s*, Cambridge 1977, Table 5.2.4, pp322-3.

[2]   Ibid, Table 5.2.2, p.318.

[3]   J. Ingram, *Geographical Mobility in Angus c 1780-1830*. Unpublished PhD, University of St Andrews 1992.

[4]   *Reports from Assistant Handloom Weavers' Commissioners*. Report by J.D. Harding on the East of Scotland. 1839. In Irish University Press Series of British Parliamentary Papers. Industrial Revolution. Textiles. 9 Shannon, Ireland.

[5]   T. Devine (ed) *Farm Servants and Labour in Lowland Scotland, 1770-1914*, Edinburgh 1984.

Chapter Four

Linen

"tradition claims it to have been a weavers' village"

The hamlet of Burnside of Dun is mainly remembered today for its weavers:

> For loom and shuttle ance went fast
> About the Burnside.
>
> But whaur are a' the weavers noo
> Wha worked the hale day lang:
> The beam and shuttle blythly drew
> Wi mony a joke and sang?[1]

wrote Elizabeth Moir, born into a family of weavers, writers and poets in the hamlet.

In 1841, ten handloom weavers are recorded as living in Burnside. Handloom weavers in rural districts tended to live in older, more primitive and cheaper cottages. Even where farm workers were benefitting from improved dwellings in the first half of the 19th century, handloom weavers were generally only able to afford houses which were of such poor quality, and built of mud or clay walls, that they would "deteriorate quickly when vacated"[2].

Handloom weaving survived in Scotland until the end of the 19th century. After 1815 and the end of the Napoleonic Wars, wages and working conditions fell rapidly following the so-called "Golden Age", leading to near starvation for many families. But in 1838 there were still 84,560 handlooms across the whole country, affording employment to many more. By 1860, the number of handloom weavers in Scotland had fallen to 19,000 and these were mainly in the "fancy trade" such as the Paisley shawl and the Dunfermline linen damask industries.

In the East of Scotland, textiles mainly meant linen, outwith the jute processing centres of Dundee and Forfar. Most linen handloom weavers lived in villages, although the towns of Angus contained many hundreds. The government inquiry into handloom weavers in the 1830s notes 8,000 linen weavers living in villages in the East of Scotland[3]. Linen handloom weavers mostly wove coarse, light cloths such as osnaburgs (often exported to the West Indies to clothe slaves), dowlas and common sheetings. These required less skill than the "fancy trade" and less strength than sailcloth. Handloom weavers were paid by the piece, and by 1838 were earning between 5s 6d and 7s 6d per week (day labourers were earning around 9s a week in this part of Angus) although real wages held up better here than in the West of Scotland and rural weavers had the chance to supplement their wages with work on the farms and with the produce of their kailyards. Probably because less skill was needed, the apprentice system had largely collapsed by the early years of the 19th century and Murray calculates that women and children made up around one third of the Scottish workforce[4].

The traditional trade of "customer" or "customary" weavers making up cloth for individual buyers or "customers" using the customer's own material could still be found in villages until the 1830s, as could "market weavers" who bought their wefts and yarn and sold the finished product themselves in the market. These weavers were often highly skilled and would have enjoyed higher incomes than those employed on piecework.

In some areas, part-time or more correctly seasonal weaving was the norm for rural weavers who would help out with farm work at certain times of the year, especially at harvest when they might even travel to more distant districts. Manufacturers who employed rural weavers are known to have complained vigorously at the delays in production caused by weavers' preference for bringing the harvest in, but country weavers were useful for producing "varieties and widths for which demand was uncertain"[5]. Agents would supply the webs and pay according to the finished length. From their wages handloom weavers, unlike factory weavers, also had to pay for fuel and lighting, starch for sizing the webs and often for pirn (bobbin) winding too. Moreover, weavers in the east of Scotland were especially apt to complain of the manufacturers' habit of arbitrarily altering the length of the ell, the traditional measure of a web of linen cloth.

The situation of rural linen handloom weavers in the "Golden Age", before the end of the Napoleonic Wars, is described rather idyllically in Headrick's *General View of the Agriculture of Angus or Forfarshire*[6]:

> I may very safely say that in Angus shire only there are employed in the linen manufacture from 20,000 to 25,000 people. Many of these reside in the towns of Dundee, Arbroath, Brechin and Forfar but many, and I believe the greater number, are scattered through the villages and the country where every one has a garden and generally an acre or two of ground. As their trade admits without prejudice of short interruptions they cultivate these little farms very successfully, greatly to the benefit of their own health and the improvement and beauty of the country. As weaving may be carried on in any place, so all ages and each sex are employed by it. The women spin, the men weave and the children who are able to do any thing are able to fill the yarn.

We know that weavers lived in Burnside from the 1790s. Did the Burnside weavers work on their own account, as customer or market weavers, or were they employed by manufacturers or agents? Customer weavers tended to be found in ones or twos in the countryside, not in groups as large as in Burnside. By the 1830s, moreover, this traditional way of working was rarely found in easily accessible areas such as Dun. Almost all the Burnside weavers came from outwith the parish – would they have moved to the hamlet to be self-employed alongside potential competitors? Farms in the parish were all improved, with the old rigs enclosed into fields by this time. Flax, a notoriously unreliable crop which depleted soil nutrients, is not mentioned in either of the Statistical Accounts for Dun. Would the farmers have been prepared to allow the Burnsiders land for flax[7]? Could the land available for crops in the hamlet have been enough for flax as well as vegetables and – perhaps – grazing for a few cattle? Would the weavers have had the resources - land, time, labour – to prepare the flax through the many stages required before the spun yarn could be woven? Market weavers would have found Burnside very far from the nearest cloth market in Dundee. However, it has been – so far – impossible to ascertain how the Burnside weavers were employed, and by whom, and in any case this probably changed over the lifetime of the settlement. In view of the number of weavers known to have been living in Burnside at the time of the 1841 Census, it is perhaps noteworthy that the New Statistical Account, written in the early 1830s, makes no specific mention of weavers amongst the nine men it identifies in the parish as "chiefly employed in trade, manufacturers or handicraft"[8].

William Jolly's biography of the weaver botanist John Duncan (1794–1881) gives an heroic view of handloom weaving in eastern Scotland. After explaining how the work of the weaver stimulated the mind and the body: "the feet work the 'treddles', the fingers tie the thread while the eye is ever on the alert to see that all goes well in the countless intricacies of the cords", Jolly continues:

> Weavers then formed, as a whole, a remarkable class of men – intelligent and observant of the progress of events at home and abroad; devoted to politics – strongly or wildly radical if not tainted with revolutionary sentiments after the intoxication of the first French Revolution; great talkers when they gathered together in the street or public-house, during the intervals of work; intensely theological, often religious, well-versed in all the intricacies of Calvinism, severest critics of the minister's discourses and keenest of heresy-hunters.[9]

We know enough about the lives of some of the individual men and women who worked at the loom in Burnside to be able to speculate that they could have recognised this account. Amongst them were kirk elders, a poet and a teacher.

The weaver Robert Smith, is probably the Robert Smith who lived in Burnside of Balnillo at the time of his daughter Elizabeth's baptism in 1792. However the OPR also records weavers living at Dun's Mill, Tayock Bridge and "Balnillo", so Burnside at this point was in no way exceptional as a place where weavers lived. In May 1837, he was ordained a kirk elder. It is possible that Robert Smith may have worked as a customer weaver, which would explain his elevation to such a respectable position. Nevertheless, he died a pauper, in 1847. His youngest son, James, was one of only two Burnside weavers to have been born in the parish.

The attraction of Burnside to weavers from elsewhere is unclear. And was the land deliberately leased to weavers to establish a pool of essential seasonal labour for the nearby farms? Even when the hamlet's recorded population was at its peak, in the 1841 Census, only ten of the 25 people with occupations were linen handloom weavers. However three of the weavers had wives who may also have worked at the loom – this Census did not usually list occupations of married women. Three of the weavers were teenagers and likely to be semi-skilled at best.

Unusually for a settlement with such a high turnover of inhabitants, all of the weavers living in Burnside in 1861 had been there in 1841: William Kinloch, John Mitchell, Homer Cruikshank, Elizabeth Moir and her daughter Isobella, together with the grown-up daughters of Christina Lindsey, and James Smith. By 1861, when handloom weaving was in its death-throes, most of the men were elderly: their average age was 65 although all but one of the women (Elizabeth Moir) was under 40. By the 1871 Census, only Elizabeth Moir, now aged 71, was described as a weaver while her son-in-law James Smith was working as a farm labourer and Homer Cruikshank appeared as a retired weaver.

Homer Cruikshank (1791–1881) was born the second son and youngest child of James Cruikshank, subtenant at Arrat's Mill on the River South Esk, and Isabel Skea. With his wife Isabella – they were married in Dun in 1820 – Homer has the distinction of having spent the longest time in Burnside – around sixty years. From the early 1830s, he is found amongst the lists of heads of households who were regular communicants at Dun Kirk. He was also the most entrepreneurial inhabitant. In the 1841 census he is described as a grocer. Ten years later he is a carrier and sharing his house, which boasted three rooms with windows, with two young lodgers, both linen handloom weavers. By 1861, Homer is 69 and one of the weavers has left but he has four new lodgers, all young ditchers from Ireland as well as a handloom weaver, James Smith, who was probably his brother-in-law. At this stage of his life he is a weaver once more. Homer's ventures into grocery and then the carrying trade are rather intriguing. It is possible that he was in fact a master weaver who employed those of his lodgers who were weavers, and that he also acted as an agent supplying wefts to other weavers in the hamlet. A line in Elizabeth Moir's poem hints at this role:

> "I see auld Homer noddin' past
> His pirn creel by his side"

Filling pirns (bobbins) for weavers was an occupation for the old, women and children. The Poor Law Inquiry of 1844 mentions several very old paupers in Brechin who earned pittances by filling pirns with yarn (and who were too old to spin). These would then be distributed to weavers, or customer weavers would buy them. Perhaps Homer acted as agent between spinners, pirn winders and weavers in the hamlet. Alternatively, he may have been a market weaver.

Homer was admitted to Sunnyside Lunatic Asylum at the end of December 1879, suffering from senile dementia, dying nine days later, aged 87 (according to the death certificate; 88 according to his baptismal record) – a good age for his times. His death certificate gives few details and his wife is not named. There is no evidence that Homer and Isabella, who died four years later, ever had any children. Isabella's occupation is only mentioned in the 1881 census, when she is described as a retired farm servant.

Elizabeth Moir or Stool (or Stoole) (1799–1880) was the last handloom weaver in Burnside and we know a great deal about her and her family. Her brother John, also a weaver, wrote a large number of letters to his family and friends recording the family's history over 100 years, from the middle of the 18th century. By great good fortune, one of John's sons, James Stool, collected these and a typed copy of the manuscript has been lodged in Montrose Museum[10].

The Stool family lived in Menmuir parish in the 18th century. John and Elizabeth's paternal grandfather Peter and their father James were weavers. Throughout his long life, James also taught children, as Peter had done. Peter and James both married servant girls and they lived in various places in Menmuir and around Brechin, sometimes employing two journeymen weavers. When John, the author of the letters, was born, his father James was teaching at a school in Dunlappie, near Edzell.

John describes his father as "of a lively, cheerful disposition, being blessed with a temper not easily ruffled." However, his "High Calvinist" views got him into trouble with the local farmers on more than one occasion: he took to writing letters against their "balling [football] and drinking" and leaving them in public places such as the North Water Bridge on Sundays where they were found by the parishioners on their way to church. Below is an extract from one of them, which interestingly emphasises economic rather than moral or spiritual arguments against these practices. His attack led indirectly to his losing his post at Dunlappie school.

How foolish to see a company of farming gentlemen and their vices so very often meeting together and eating and drinking to excess wasting the substance you should lay up for your children coming after you and often times rendering yourselves unfit to go home to our own houses without a guide and ready to stammer in to any pit or pond near your way and sometimes so heated with spirits that your judgement leaves you to that degree that when you are home you are unfit to manage any of your business either within or without doors. But perhaps you will say. – We only waste that which is our own. Maybe, but perhaps you were the better of friends before you who were careful of their substance that their offspring might live comfortably and ought you not to have the same regard for those coming of or after you; beside by your practice you set an example of wasting before your posterity the habit of which won't be easily shaken off. But it is well known also that some of you who have followed these extravagancies have wasted that which had been entrusted in your hands by some of your neighbours. But the folly of the practice under review will appear farther still than this. Your feasting and high living reaches the ears of the proprietors of your farms. O says he, my land is not half rented yet. These tenants of mine live as well if not better than I do myself; as soon as there is an opportunity I must have an advance rent and thus your successors pay for your folly.

So I conclude this paper subscribing myself

Christian Brother.

John attended his father's school at Dunlappie, and at the age of twelve, in 1807, was sent to work for a relative who was a carrier in Montrose. At fourteen he started as an apprentice weaver with his father and also helped at the school. As a journeyman, he worked with other masters in the area until at the age of 25 he was able to work on his own account as a "customary" weaver. This kind of work dwindling, and his parents becoming frail, he tried school teaching at Sauchieburn where there was a large dissenting meeting house and school but, unable to make a living, he took a job as foreman at a Montrose linen factory. He had learned fancy weaving in Fettercairn and "grew expert at making drafts and cardings of any kind, which is of great use to me." He mentions, almost in passing, three books he wrote on weaving. A solitary young man, fond of rural walks, he studied mathematics and religion in his spare time, working on an index to the Bible. At the age of 40, at Sauchieburn, he met and married Barbara Strachan, a flax spinner employed at Craigo Mill, and originally from Aberdeen.

Although much more fortunate in life, especially as a youngster, John Stool's life has many echoes of that of his contemporary John Duncan, the self-taught botanist and astronomer, who spent his life as a rural weaver in Aberdeenshire. The following letter, written when John Stool was 39, provides an insight into what concerned and interested him – nature, memories of childhood and youth, religion and intellectual self-improvement (and is a good example of his slightly awkward prose style):

> 3 Sept 1834. I took a journey to see the places where I spent my flowering spring and part of my summer's strength. As I passed along the road from Sauchieburn to Brechin, I beheld the reapers busy cutting down and taking in the fruits of the earth, for another year's supply to the inhabitants of the country. The fading season is come, all those things that lately appeared blooming, are now decaying. A fine emblem of the shortness and uncertainties of life.
>
> I left Brechin and passed along the Dunlappie road. When at Lummington, I looked around me and thought on the changes in that part of the country since I first knew it. Many of my old companions removed to other parts of the country. My father came to this place in 1808 and he, my mother, a brother and sister, with whom I spent the precious years of youth, no longer behold the things that are done under the sun. The house is now decaying in which I learned the art of weaving and gained many a pound by hard work and slept soundly many a night after the labours of the day. ... I visited my chair that I had cut out of the Brae at the edge of the Burn, at which I spent many a Sabbath afternoon with my old companions Theron and Aspasio, Booth, Newton, etc. When seated on this chair which was as soft as a sofa, I had nothing to molest me except, sometimes, the busy emmet [ant] came running over me in search of food. ... I contemplated the many changes that have taken place during the last 30 years.

The Glen, Woodside, where there were houses all demolished and my companions scattered to the four quarters of the world. The Braes remain as they were formerly, covered over with broom and fen and many useful herbs, all growing together, without cultivation from gardeners and the little walks are still to be seen, aslant their sides formed originally by the hares and sheep tripping along.

In letter 13, John recounts the story of his younger sister Elizabeth. She was born on 17 December 1799 in the parish of Stracathro and was "weakly in her youth". She was in service in half a dozen farms and houses in the area. In 1825 she married James Moir, a shoemaker, and went to live in St Cyrus. According to John, he was "not healthy at [his trade] and he wrought at salmon fishing in summer". After five years, they moved to Dun, living first at Fordes (Fordhouse) and later at Muir of Dun, where James died of fever, on 8 August 1837. Elizabeth was left at the age of 37 with five children aged from one to eleven, and a baby on the way, and at that stage probably moved to Burnside. John sums up his sister's subsequent life – "My sister and her children have been blest with ordinary health and she works for the most part at the loom." Thus John dismisses Elizabeth. Their older sister Mary who went to India with her soldier husband and wrote 100 hymns is awarded a rather more appreciative account.

Elizabeth and James were married by a dissenting minister and all their children were baptised at Sauchieburn, although the baptisms are also recorded in Dun OPR, with a note "the Parents James Moir and Elisabeth Stoole were Anabaptists".

Elizabeth was a writer of verse, and John quotes her lament for Menmuir, written in 1832 after the death of her father:

But when I first did there arrive
Parents I then had family five
But in the parish now remains,
None but what the churchyard contains.
And this makes Menmuir now no more,
The same to me as heretofore.
No monument remains to tell
Where this my father long did dwell.
But living monuments there are
Who still like me his name revere.
Our house was humble, poor and mean,
But always peaceful, calm, serene…

In 1841 Elizabeth was living in Burnside with four of her children and the oldest, Isobel or Isobella, then fifteen (see Plate 12), was living next door as a female servant with a young handloom weaver, Ann Mitchell. George, then thirteen, was probably working elsewhere. At the age of fourteen, George was killed in an accident on a farm while playing in the wheel house (threshing building) and Elizabeth lost her daughter Jean a few years later at the age of eleven in 1848. By the next Census, only her sixteen-year-old daughter, also Elizabeth (see Plate 11), and Alexander, then fifteen and still, unusually, at school, were living with her. She is described as a linen handloom weaver and pauper and had appeared in the Heritors' Minute Book for 1845 and 1846 as one of the eight resident paupers, receiving 4s/- monthly. In 1861, the household consisted of Elizabeth and Isobella, both working at the loom, and Isobella's two children, John and Elisabeth Young. In December 1848, Isobella had married a tailor, James Young, but he died before 1858. The 1861 census is the first to give the number of rooms with windows in the houses. The Moir family had a three-roomed house at this stage.

Isobella married again in 1866 when she was 40. Her second husband was James Smith, the youngest son of the Elder, Robert Smith and his second wife Helen Mitchell, and by this time no longer a weaver. A year later, Isobella gave birth to a son, James Cruikshank Smith. It is conceivable that Homer and Isobella (née Smith) Cruikshank were related to the Smith family. The Cruikshanks and the Smiths were also neighbours. In 1871 Elizabeth Moir, now aged 71 and still apparently working as a weaver, was living with James and Isobella and their son in Burnside. The household also included her grandson, James McNab, her daughter Elizabeth's illegitimate child and Jane Ross, aged sixteen, a disabled pauper girl who was boarded out with the Moirs by Montrose Parochial Board. To accommodate these six people they had two rooms.

Elizabeth Moir died at Burnside on 11 June 1880, aged 80. She is buried in the churchyard at Dun and the gravestone remembers her husband James Moir and three of her children who died young – George, Jean and Alexander, who died at Gibraltar while serving with the King's Own Borderers. Soon after, James and Isobella moved to Tayock with their little group of young people (Isobella's daughter Elizabeth Young, her son Alexander, James McNab and James C Smith). Two of Elizabeth Moir's daughters moved further away: Elizabeth to Fife and Anna (see Plate 4) to Australia, where James McNab (see Plate 14) also ended up. James C Smith (see Plate 13) was made dux of Montrose Academy, went to Edinburgh University, then Oxford and later became Chief Inspector of Schools for Scotland.

John Mitchell was another weaver who taught children. In 1841, he was 50 years of age and living with his elderly mother and sister, Jean, in Burnside. John and Jean had been born in Montrose, children of George Mitchell, described as an agricultural labourer on John's death certificate, and both were unmarried. Their mother was another long-lived Burnsider, dying at the age of 88½. In 1851, John and Jean had a young relative living with them, six-year-old John Bowen, who is identified as a "Scholar at home". John Mitchell in that census is described as "handloom weaver and teacher". In 1861 he was a weaver and teacher of reading, but there were no young scholars in the house, so he may have taught some of the many children in the hamlet. In this he too followed the path of the many handloom weavers who varied their hard and monotonous toil with study and involvement in intellectual pursuits. John Mitchell, unlike several of the other male weavers who were heads of households, is not listed among the regular communicants in the Dun Kirk Session minutes, so he may have attended one of the dissenting meeting houses in the district. He died in 1863 aged 74 while visiting his niece in Airlie.

Were the Burnside weavers farm labourers who wove in the winter or weavers who helped with the harvest? Their later lives do not really help to answer this question, as the rapid decline of handloom weaving in the second half of the 19th century would have forced nearly all weavers, full- or part-time, into other occupations. Francis Brown was one of the youngest handloom weavers in 1841. Then aged fourteen he lived with his mother not in Burnside itself but in "Moor of Balnillo". Ten years later they were in Burnside and he was still weaving, but by 1861 he had become a gardener at Broomley, a large house on the Dun Estate. Elizabeth Moir's son-in-law, James Smith, appears in later censuses as an agricultural labourer. On the other hand, William Kinloch, in Burnside with his wife in the 1850s and 1860s ended his life in Bervie at the age of 80 in 1884, a cotton weaver according to his death certificate, although Bervie's mills were jute and flax. Christina Smith or Lindsey, the daughter of a crofter, lived as an agricultural labourer though the mother of weavers, according to the censuses, but died in 1863 at the age of 68 as a weaver, according to her death certificate. However, it needs to be acknowledged that census data on individual occupations is not always completely reliable.

NOTES

[1] E. Moir *The Auld Burnside, Parish of Dun, near Montrose*, no date.

[2] G. Lloyd, *Linen Handloom Weavers' Houses in Scotland: a social and architectural study*, unpublished B Arch thesis, University of Dundee, 1990.

[3] Report by J.D. Harding on the East of Scotland. In *Reports of Assistant Handloom Weavers' Commissioners*.

[4] N. Murray, *The Scottish Hand Loom Weavers 1790-1850: a social history*, Edinburgh 1978, p. 26.

[5] C. Whatley, *Onward from Osnaburgs*, Edinburgh. 1992, p. 87. The timing of the harvest often had an impact on the completion of orders.

[6] J. Headrick *op.cit*, p. 126.

[7] It has been suggested in a personal communication that farmers allowed weavers in Burnside to grow flax on the rigends.

[8] *NSA* Vol. 11, p.124.

[9] W. Jolly, *The Life of John Duncan, Scotch Weaver and Botanist*, London 1883.

[10] James Stool collected his father's letters in two books, The Stool Journals, one dealing with the family history and the second containing articles on religious controversies his father was involved in, as an active member of various non-established churches in Angus. The two books were transcribed by hand by one of the Stool family's descendants, Travis Thomas (of New South Wales, Australia) and with his permission another descendant, Robyn Hukin, typed it and lodged a copy with Montrose Museum.

Plate 1: The memorial at Burnside of Dun

Plate 2: The inscription on the memorial

Plate 3: Burnside in May

Plate 4: Dun's Dish

Plate 5: *Trinity Fair* by David Waterson (undated) from the Collections of Montrose Museum, courtesy of Angus Council, Cultural Services

Plate 6: *Linen weaver* by David Waterson (1890) from the Collections of Montrose Museum, courtesy of Angus Council, Cultural Services

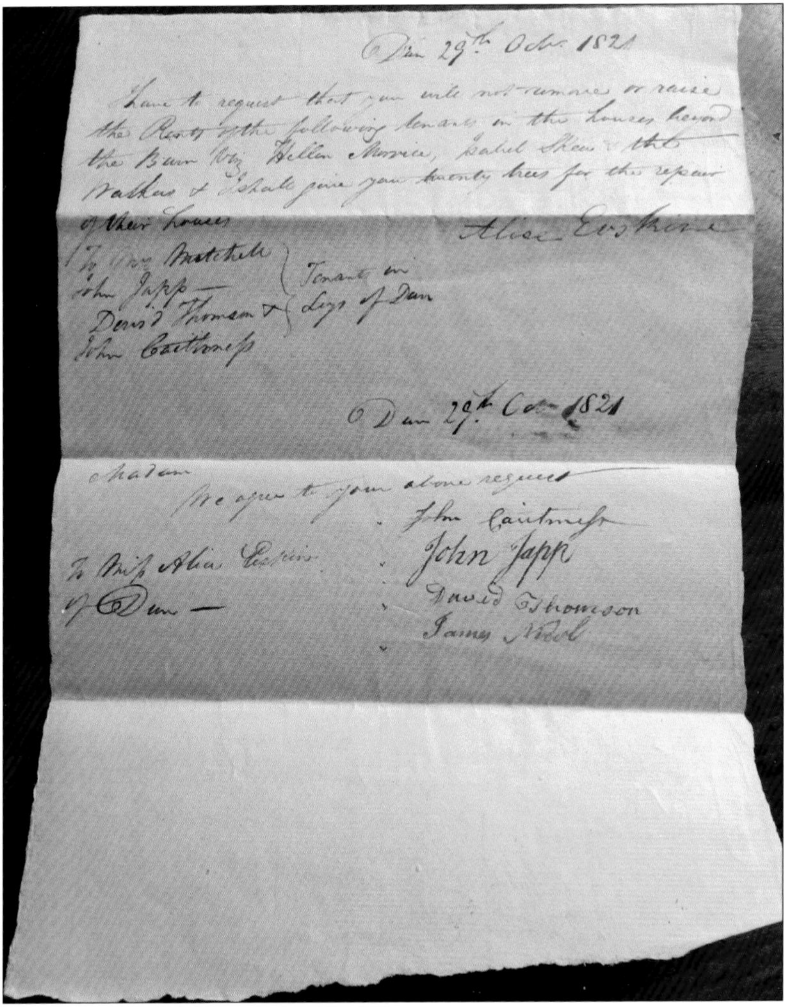

Dun 29th Octr 1821

I have to request that you will not remove or raise the Rents of the following tenants in the houses beyond the Burn Viz Hellen Morrice, Isabel Shaw & the Walkers & I shall give you twenty trees for the repair of their houses

Alice Erskine

To Wm Mitchell
John Japp
David Thomson &
John Caithness
} Tenants in Leys of Dun

Dun 29th Octr 1821

Madam

We agree to your above request

John Caithness
John Japp
David Thomson
James Nicol

To Miss Alice Erskine
of Dun —

Plate 7: Note by Alice Erskine to her tenants in Leys of Dun, 29 Oct 1821.
Photograph reproduced courtesy of the National Trust for Scotland

Plate 8: Footings of House G

Plate 9: Footbridge over the burn

Plates 10–12: The Moir Family: the daughters of Elizabeth Stool and James Moir.
Photographs reproduced courtesy of Robyn Hukin

53

Plates 13-14: The Moir Family: their grandsons, who erected the Memorial. Photographs reproduced courtesy of Montrose Academy and Robyn Hukin

Chapter Five

Cottages and kailyards

"the houses were mostly built of clay, with earthen floors and thatched roofs"

Today, all that can be seen of the ruined houses of Burnside are their outlines, marked by low piles of rounded stones (see Plate 8). Andrew Lamb, overseer on the Dun Estate, recalled in 1930 that "the houses were mostly built of clay, with earthen floors and thatched roofs"[1]. Cottages built of clay mixed with straw or heather were not uncommon in Kincardine and North Angus in the 18th and 19th centuries but references in documents to "clay biggins" or "clay walls" may in fact mean stone walls faced with clay[2]. Nevertheless, there were sources of clay in the parish and patches of clay in the neighbouring fields, and clay buildings are common in the district. A triangular district made up of the villages of Laurencekirk, Luthermuir and Hillside contains a large number of earthen buildings. Very recently, a schoolhouse built of clay and straw in 1835 near Montrose was restored by the National Trust for Scotland[3].

Clay was not always cheaper than stone, but clay houses were more likely to be found where stone was scarce. This does not seem to have been the case in Burnside as there is a good-sized quarry in the Den of Dun, not far from the hamlet. An alternative to clay could have been turf, or turf divots taken from the adjacent muir and faced with drystone. The Leys of Duns leases of 1801 (see below) indicate that at least some of the houses were built with turf. The quantity of stones still visible at the site does not really help in deciding how the walls were built. Clay and bool, where rounded river stones are set in the clay and the walls built up with formwork (shuttering) is another possibility. That there was plenty of clay in the vicinity is attested by the tileworks at Mains of Dun, which employed thirty-eight workers in 1861. Pointing with lime and limewashing of the walls completed the work.[4]

The cottages of the poor were commonly roofed with a thatch of straw, heather or broom. Clay walls in any case could not usually support the grey Angus slates[5]. Broom could have been gathered from the nearby muir, and straw presumably from the farms: Jane Anne Duthie recalls that in the 1870s "they were a' thackit but ane"[6]. Inside, they would probably, like most houses of the poor built before 1850, have had no ceilings, but have been open to the roof [7]. The walls inside and out would have been coated with lime and there would have been small windows, probably without glass.

In the early 19th century, Headrick noted that cottages "have been greatly improved of late year. They are generally built with stone and clay with clay floors and thatched roofs. A house of this sort thirty feet in length and sixteen in breadth over walls may be constructed for about L 15 [£15]"[8]. Nevertheless, Fenton and Walker make the point that in the first half of the century farm workers and other rural workers were often housed in appalling conditions[9], even while farmers were moving into improved farmhouses with glazed windows and two storeys. Plans for new and enlarged farm steadings could include bothies for farm servants next door to, and considerably less spacious than, the stables or the henhouse. It was not until the 1850s that concerns about the moral degeneration occasioned by the overcrowding of rural workers' homes as well as health fears drove a nationwide effort to provide better quality housing. However, it is unlikely that a settlement of mere day labourers would have attracted the attentions of local farmers more concerned to retain farm servants. Headrick further notes:

> Another kind of cottages are very frequent in various parts of this county These are constructed by weavers and other kinds of tradesmen upon allotments of waste land which they occupy either upon a long lease or a feu. Some of these are only temporary erections built of turf with a mixture of stones and are meant to accommodate their families and their looms until they get their lots of land reduced to cultivation … Neighbourhood to a town or to a public road is a great inducement to set down these cottages and they are also much influenced by their position in respect to a peat moss or other fuel[10].

We may assume that housing conditions in Burnside started comfortless and got worse throughout the 19th century. In the Charter Room in House of Dun, there are four identical tacks (leases) for Leys of Dun dated 1801[11]. Each tenant was to have a house built at John Erskine's expense: £4 in cash and 6 bolls of lime "to teeth the walls and also wood for cupples for the same." For the "houses beyond the burn" the proprietor bound himself to supply "one tree for every four feet in length for roofing … when they require it." These houses were in what became Burnside of Dun and are probably the three shown on the Ordnance Survey First edition map (1865), almost on the north bank of the burn (Houses I, J and K on Map 4). These houses seem to have been the first to disappear later in the century. The tack further grants each tenant "liberty to cast feal [turf] and divot on the muir for building houses so long as any part of it shall remain unappropriated to any other purpose [ie not enclosed or planted]". There is a further note signed by the redoubtable Alice Erskine, laird of Dun, and addressed to the four tenants of the Leys, dated 1821 (Plate 7) : "I have to request that you will not remove or raise the Rents of the following tenants in the houses beyond the Burn viz Hellen Morrice, Isabel Skea and the Walkers and I shall give you twenty trees for the repair of their houses." If there were three houses and the trees were only for the roofs, each house could have been around twenty feet in length.

It is most probable the houses were built by the people themselves, either cutting and carting turf from the muir or mixing clay from a nearby source with field stones or straw and building the walls, with or without shuttering, layer by layer, allowing each course to dry thoroughly before adding the next. Bruce Walker describes turf building as "a community effort": "the master turf builder was often an elderly member of the community … with a reputation built up from years of experience"[12]. This man would find the best quality turf and decide when and how to cut it, and how high the walls should go at the end of each day, before being left to dry. As the 1801 tacks make clear, wood for the rooftrees was supplied by the proprietor, and he may have provided wood for doors too. Robyn Hukin, genealogist and descendant of the Moir family, has provided the following anecdote:

> I was interested to read your description of how the houses were built of clay and straw and it occurred to me this may have been how my great-great-grandmother Anna Moir [see Plate 10] knew how to build her wattle and daub family home with her husband in South Australia. As the 2nd eldest surviving child with her father dying when she was seven, I imagine she was required to do a lot of work to help her widowed mother, including house repairs. I do know though from people who set about recreating houses in Beltana, South

Australia, that there was a sort of woven inner wall of saplings. When I first visited the outback town where she lived the locals all told me she used to get an apronful of stones each time she left the house and plug them into spaces between these sticks, and then clay and straw was pushed between the stones. The floor was paved with large flag stones as found in the vicinity. Certainly there was no shortage of stones in the area [ie Burnside] when I visited, nor clay. Anyway, wattle and daub was a very common housebuilding method here too. Anna's husband was from a Glasgow tenement so I suspect he didn't have to do a lot of housebuilding!

Clay or turf cottages may have been more comfortable than one might expect, so long as they were carefully maintained. In 1813, such houses were described (although not by an occupant) as "warm and impervious to wind and weather, looking well when whitened with lime plaster"[13]. Walls built of clay could be fully load-bearing and last for many years if properly looked after. It is not possible to determine how well the Burnside houses were built or maintained except that most seem to have survived, one way or another, till the 1870s.

One house was not built in this way. The house beside the Kirk track known in the 20th century as the Beadle's house – it was occupied by the Church Officer and his family at the time of the 1901 census – was built of stone, with a roof made of slate, too heavy for clay houses. It seems that the Beadle's house was not strictly part of the settlement. The *Brechin Advertiser* described it in 1930 as "a pendicle apart from the hamlet proper, but adjacent to it." Part of the present day building was once a small semi-detached home, which still shows signs of having been built of clay and bool.

The Ordnance Survey First Edition 25 inch to the mile map (1865) shows nine roofed buildings and one unroofed building. This appears to represent seven detached dwellings and ten semi-detached or terraced dwellings in the area of Burnside (see Map 4). Five of the dwellings are in Burnside of Dun, the remainder on Balnillo land (part of the Balwyllo estate). The 1861 Census lists eighteen households, five on the Dun estate. We do not know in more detail who lived where as the census enumerator gave each house a number only for the purpose of the Census, and these numbers changed from Census to Census.

Headrick describes the system of cottage settlements succinctly:

> [T]hese villages have been chiefly set down upon tracts of land, which, at their commencement, were wholly waste and unproductive, so as hardly to be worth a shilling *per* acre of rent. They have been chiefly built on lots of land, varying in extent from less than one to five or six acres, which are either held in leases of a hundred years or in perpetuity, at a rent, the average of which is 40s *per* acre. These original lots are afterwards subdivided, as the demand increases for building new houses; or they may be sold or mortgaged, being to all intents and purposes real property. But when those which are held in perpetual feu are so disposed of, the landlord is entitled to a year's rent of the actual value, for admitting singular successors into possession, according to the old feudal ideas concerning the *delectus personae*, which a superior was held to possess in the admission of a vassal. The effect of these villages is not only to bring waste land into cultivation, but to enhance the value of the contiguous land. They relieve the farmer from the necessity of keeping unnecessary hands upon his farm, as he can always have what labourers he wants in any emergency. This increases the amount of his disposable produce, and enables him to pay a higher rent. The only bar to their increase is scarcity of fuel; and were the county intersected by canals a considerable proportion of it would become a continued village.[14]

In Burnside, the extent of the land attached to each house varied considerably. The Ordnance Survey First Edition *Book of reference to the Plan of the Parish of Dun*[15] of 1864 gives the extent of the plots of land occupied by individual houses and groups of houses and their gardens or kailyards. One house (F on Map 4) had around half an acre. House H, south of the burn and also detached, also had half an acre of land, but this was shared between two households. Five houses at the core of the settlement (B, C, D, E and G) accommodating ten separate households shared just under two acres of land, or around one-fifth of an acre per household. Another group of houses (I, J, K), in the eastern, Dun, portion, had just under one acre for four households. House A had one sixteenth of an acre. However, the *Book of Reference* lists nearly nine acres of arable land (together with part of the burn and part of

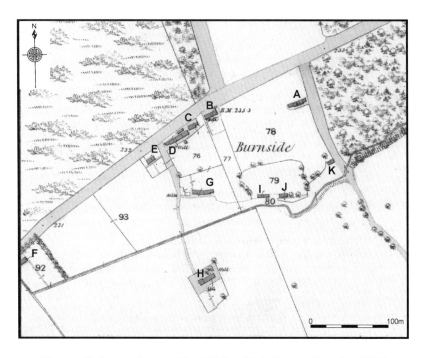

Map 4: Ordnance Survey First Edition 25 inches to the mile (1865)
Forfarshire Sheet XXVII (detail).
Courtesy of the National Library of Scotland.
Letters A to H refer to buildings, not individual houses.

the road) within the hamlet as unallocated, so the total acreage available to
the cottagers may in fact have been nearly thirteen acres. A quarter of an
acre of arable land would be very adequate for vegetables and fruit for a
household, and much more generous than the yards of farmworkers' tied
cottages which were generally between 100 square yards and one eighth of an
acre. J.C. Loudon, the ardent evangelist of democratic gardening in the early
decades of the 19th century, considered an eighth of an acre an ideal size for
a cottage garden[16]. On the other hand, these gardens were not nearly as big
as pendicles. David Walsh, Angus local history investigator, has remarked:

> If these are pendicles, I would have normally expected a strip
> of land to be placed in front or behind the dwelling. In this

case, there would not have been much land in the centre to allow any degree of self-sufficiency for the inhabitants, but the 6" to the mile map does indicate fenced off areas in the central area associated with most of the dwellings. The burn (a drainage channel from the Dish used subsequently for the Mill of Dun) would have made an attached strip of land difficult for the southern cottages. ... Flooding of the site might have been a problem after rain or snow melt. In such a circumstance, a central dished area might have served as a flood buffer. Ducks and geese might have used such an area and been a part of the inhabitants self-sufficiency.

Pendicles were normally feued and there is no documentary evidence of feuing by either the Erskines of Dun or the Carnegys of Craigo. Whether the unallocated land included pasture for cows is not known, although in other weaver villages each household had a cow, tended by a communal herd, or Tuttie. It is possible that the Burnsiders were given a rig or two in the farmers' fields for potatoes or even flax as was common throughout the East of Scotland. Each household probably kept a pig, near the cottage.

From 1861, census enumerators were required to record the number of rooms with windows in each house. In Burnside in 1861 three of the houses had one room with a window, eight had two and seven had three. Of course houses also may have had rooms without windows, for example attics, loomsheds and byres. The Ordnance Survey First Edition 25 inch to the mile map (1865) shows several of the buildings with small extensions at one or both ends. House G today shows evidence of having had a byre at its western end. Some may have had rooms, of a kind, in the roof space. The weaver John Duncan lived for ten years in the village of Auchleven in Aberdeenshire in a roof space seven foot long, with only room to stand up under the ridge and no window but a hole with a piece of wood to cover it[17].

Two-roomed cottages were the most common. This was also the situation throughout Scotland: in 1861, 37% of families lived in two rooms, and as late as 1911, more than half the population lived in one- or two-roomed homes. Overcrowding was appreciably less in rural areas, however, than in the cities of the time. Nationally, the average number of people living in single-roomed homes was five but in Burnside in 1861 only one couple lived in a single-roomed house, the others of this type being occupied by lone inhabitants. In the same census, several large families lived in two-roomed houses, but by 1881 such families were living in three rooms, the falling population allowing the larger families to occupy the larger houses.

	1861	1871	1881	1891
	No. of houses	No. of houses	No of houses	No. of houses
1 roomed houses	3	1	0	1
2-roomed houses	8	10	4	3
3-roomed houses	5	0	3	1
average no. of persons per room	1.5	2.33	1.5	1.5
uninhabited houses	1	4	1	1
total houses	17	15	8	6

Source: Census Enumeration Books for Dun

Table 5.1 Burnside of Dun house occupancy 1861–1891

The most overcrowded homes in Burnside were those of the largest families: Thomas and Catherine Pender and three of their children, together with a lodger, lived in two rooms in 1861 as did James and Ann Harper and their five children. Some households were three generations strong. In 1871 Elizabeth Moir together with her daughter Isabella's family and Jane Ross the young epileptic boarder were living three to a room and John and Margaret Watt, their widowed daughter and three small grandchildren were also in two rooms. But Homer and Isabella Cruikshank's home seems overcrowded too, with five boarders in three rooms in 1861. It is possible of course that children and lodgers slept in the attic or a shed, without windows, like John Duncan.

Weavers' houses in the countryside were usually single-storey, with two or three rooms. The loomshop might be a room in the house or in an outhouse or extension with a peind (sloping) roof, especially if there were more than one loom. A cool, damp atmosphere was essential for lubricating the flax fibres, so earthen floors into which the treadles might be sunk were usual. If there was a window it would be kept tight shut to maintain the damp atmosphere. The flax produced dust and oil as well as harmful fumes.

Labourers' houses might be just as unhealthy. Cottages in Angus and Perthshire were described as late as the 1890s as "in many cases far from satisfactory: some of them only have one room, a division being made by the furniture … some are sunk in a clay soil and are consequently damp, standing below the level of the ground"[18]. We may imagine that this was an accurate depiction of many of the cottages in Burnside.

A garden or kailyard for rural workers was less of a hobby than an essential means of feeding the family. It also kept the people, especially the weavers, healthier than urban workers. Alexander Fenton in *Scottish Country Life* notes that cottage gardens were unknown in Scotland before the 19th century, but that rural folk then quickly took up gardening, raising carrots, leeks, onions, potatoes and kail for broth, also growing rhubarb and berry bushes for jellies and jams (for which however, large quantities of sugar would be required)[19]. The Burnsiders may have mainly sown potatoes but we know that, latterly at least, they also grew soft fruit: to this day, gooseberry bushes can be seen in several places among the ruins. All those who have written or spoken about Burnside recall the gardens, the fruit trees and bushes. Jane Anne Duthie wrote of "a stragglin' rose bush tryin' to force its way through the rubbish; some black currant bushes and honeysuckle and here and there plants that had wont to be used for healin' purposes – 'healin' blades' they used to be ca'd"[20]. Mr Ewan, born in 1906 the son of the blacksmith at Dun, told the author in 1977 of the apple and pear trees still standing when he used to go there. Keeping fruit trees does suggest both an expectation of long-term residence and the ability to tend them.

So far, no evidence of rents – how much, if any, and paid to whom – has come to light for the earlier part of the story of Burnside. In 1843, the Minister's testimony to the Royal Commission on the Poor Law included the information that labourers in the parish paid rents of £1–£2 a year. In the 1890s James Patterson, the General Merchant, paid £5 per annum in rent, while the Beadle was paying £4, which was also the standard nominal rent for tied farm cottages. However other cottages in the Balnillo portion had a rents of £2 and £1, suggesting something much more basic in the way of accommodation[21].

The County Sanitary Inspector, appointed under the Public Health (Scotland) Act of 1889, reports in his first Annual Report (1891) that while farm servants are now better housed, the declining number of day labourers are living in villages blighted by empty houses (many abandoned after the end of rural handloom weaving), reduced rents and "general dilapidation and the owners unable to keep what had once been tidy cottages in a comfortable and healthy state of repair."[22] Villages without mains water or sewerage, such as Burnside, were "often in a filthy state and detrimental to the health of the inhabitants". In fact there were no drains in any of the rural areas of Forfarshire at that time, "hence all slops and other foul water are usually either deposited in ashpits or thrown into roadside ditches"[23]. Conditions like this make the desertion of the settlement by younger, employed inhabitants easier to understand. They left only the very old and the sick behind.

NOTES

[1]   *The Montrose Review* 2 May 1930.

[2]   A. Fenton and B. Walker, *The Rural Architecture of Scotland*, Edinburgh 1981, p.85.

[3]   The National Trust for Scotland. Buildings. *Conservation of Earth Schoolhouse Completed.* Available at http://www.nts.org.uk/Buildings/LHIS/Current/ (accessed 18/11/2013)

[4]   B. Walker and C. McGregor, *Earth Structures and Construction in Scotland. Historic Scotland Technical Advice Note 6*, Edinburgh 1996, p.67.

[5]   Fenton and Walker, *op cit*, p.79.

[6]   Duthie, *op cit*, p.122.

[7]   Ibid, p.32.

[8]   Headrick, *op cit*, p.136.

[9]   Fenton and Walker, *op cit*, p.143.

[10]   Headrick, *op cit*, p.138.

[11]   Tacks of David Thomson, William Walker, John Mitchell and Elizabeth Baillie, all Leys of Dun, 1801 NRAS 4346/9/2,4,5 and 15.

[12]   B. Walker, *Scottish Turf Construction. Historic Scotland Technical Advice Note 30*, Edinburgh 2006, p.5.

[13]   G. Robertson, General View of the Agriculture of the County of Kincardine, London 1810, p.201

[14]   Headrick, *op cit*, pages 211-212.

[15]   Ordnance Survey First Edition.

[16]   J. C. Loudon, *The Manual of Cottage Gardening and Husbandry*, 1830, cited in J. Uglow, *A Little History of British Gardening*, London 2004, p.196.

[17]   Jolly, *op cit*, p.111.

18 *Records of the County Medical Officer of Health*, Forfar, 1891, p.10

19 A. Fenton, *Scottish Country Life*, Edinburgh 1999.

20 Duthie, *op cit*, p.124.

21 *Valuation Rolls for Forfarshire* 1891-2, 1892-3.

22 *Records of the County Medical Officer of Health*, p.12.

23 Ibid, p.9.

Chapter Six

The parish of Dun

"the Parish is altogether rural"

The 1861 census enumeration books for Dun provide a snapshot of the parish and its economy. The total population was 765, mostly farm workers and their families. Trades represented included corn milling, tile manufacturing at Mains of Dun, where the farmer employed 38 workers, salmon fishing and weaving. In addition there were a parochial teacher and another private teacher, a tollkeeper, three railway porters and a station "agent" at Bridge of Dun Railway Station, three shoemakers, seven blacksmiths, a mole catcher, estate workers such as gardeners, coachmen and one gas fitter. Only six inhabitants are described as paupers, and the parish appears, with its two elegant mansions, House of Dun and Langley Park, and the large farms of Mains of Dun, Balwyllo and Gilrivie, prosperous and thriving.

The four biggest landowners were the heritors, responsible for the funding of the church and the school, including the minister's and schoolteacher's salaries and, along with the Kirk Session, for the Poors Fund. The heritor families throughout the 19th century were the Erskines of Dun (later the Kennedy-Erskines), the Carnegys of Craigo, the Cruikshanks of Langley Park and the Campbells of Stracathro. The Erskines pulled down the kirk and replaced it with the present building, judged "hideous" by Violet Jacob[1]. Later in the century, these families were often absent for most of the year, sometimes leasing their mansions to "gentlemen" tenants.

According to the 1855–6 Valuation Roll for the county, the most valuable farms were Mains of Dun, whose tenant David Crowe paid £1200 in rent to the Erskines; Balwyllo and Balnillo which gave Thomas McPherson Grant of Craigo over £900[2] a year; and Glenskenno, belonging to the same proprietor and let out for nearly £600 a year.

Following the amalgamations or "engrossments" of tenancies of the late 18th and early 19th centuries, there seems to have been very little change in the size and the value of farms. In the mid 1870s, at the beginning of the agricultural depression (which probably affected this area relatively little), Mains of Dun and Balwyllo and Balnillo were still paying the same rent as twenty years earlier.

The high status of the large tenant farmers in the 19th century is still visible: large farmhouses of this date, with landscaped grounds, overlook the Basin at Mains of Dun, Balwyllo and Gilrivie, the steading buildings carefully hidden from these mansions behind walls and shrubberies.

The civic institutions of the parish were the Kirk, overseen by the Kirk Session, the Parochial Board (from 1846) and the School Board (from 1873). In each case, we find the same landowners and biggest tenant farmers occupying all or nearly all the places, taking the chair and setting the agenda. In fact, the tendency for landed interests to run the parish seemed to strengthen during the 19th century.

Until the middle of the century, there were at least two weavers serving as elders on Dun Kirk Session. These were Robert Smith and Robert Miln both from Burnside. Robert Smith died a pauper in 1847 and the Kirk Session paid out £2 6s 6½d for his funeral, which was more than double the sum usually paid for pauper funerals. After Robert Smith's death no more tradesmen were elected as elders until the very end of the century – all were farmers.

Parochial Boards, set up under the Poor Law Act of 1845 to administer poor relief, were elected under "a complicated system of votes which favoured owners of property and excluded most of the poor"[3], although they were still heavily influenced by the Kirk Session which was tasked in any case with the disbursement of relief. Only minutes of the Dun Parochial Board from 1889 onwards survive, and these tell us that in 1890 the Chairman was the Minister, while the other members were Cruikshank of Langley Park, two tenant farmers and a wright. In 1894, the Board was replaced by a Parish Council and once again the larger farmers dominated.

When the School Board was first formed in 1873 under the terms of the Education Act, its members, elected by all occupiers of property, including women, worth £4 in annual rent, were the Minister of Glamis, recently of Dun, Augustus Cruikshank of Langley Park, and three farmers, including the tenant of Mains of Dun. The following three elections saw all the landowners taking their places on the Board in turn together with an assortment of the larger tenant farmers. The chair was invariably taken by a landowner.

The enthusiasm of these gentlemen (and two ladies at different times) for service on the School Board may perhaps be explained by the funding of public education: the School Board set the education rate (3d in the £ in 1880). This, together with modest government grants and the scholars' fees until 1890, had to pay for the school, the schoolmaster's house, the salaries of two full-time teachers and a singing teacher, equipment and eventually schoolbooks[4].

The powerful grip of landowners and large farmers over rural society in the 19th century is well known. But "[o]n Sundays the churches held the country in thrall for Christ"[5]. Sermons, church government and schisms were foremost in the concerns and thoughts of many working people throughout the 19th century. John Stool writes slightly disapprovingly of his mother that she "was not so strict on Church Government [as his much admired father]. She delighted to read Harvey Newton but never paid much attention to Church Order or Christian Fellowship". His letters on his family history are interspersed with long disquisitions on all these topics. At the close of the century, Jane Anne Duthie, the author of our only contemporary description of Burnside, kept a diary almost exclusively devoted to accounts of her thoughts and conversations about religion, anxieties about leading a Christian life and the spiritual health of her family[6].

Church attendance seems to have been quite high in Dun in the first half of the 19th century. The population of the parish in 1831 was 514 of whom perhaps one third were children under fourteen. Every year from 1834 to the Disruption of 1843 the Kirk Session recorded the names of all the male heads of families who were regular communicants. Between 60 and 70 names appeared on these lists each year. Assuming wives, adult offspring and other adult relations accompanied the paterfamilias to Church every Sunday, up to 200 adults were thus regular churchgoers perhaps representing one half to two-thirds of the adult population. This seems a high rate of regular attendance, especially as rural churchgoing tended to be lower than in the towns in Scotland at this time. The Kirk Session minutes name ten to twelve Burnsiders as regular communicants each year and, over the nine-year period, a total of 24 men who lived in Burnside and the nearby settlements of Muir of Dun and Muir of Balnillo. Of these, nine appear in the lists in six or more of these years: John Young (blacksmith), John Jack (labourer), Homer Cruikshank (weaver), David Strachan (weaver), Alexander Robert (mason), Alexander Steel (labourer), David Robert (labourer), Robert Smith (weaver) and Robert Miln or Milne (weaver). The last two were also elders, as we have seen.

Following the Disruption, regular church attendance in the parish, as measured by the numbers of regular communicants recorded in the Kirk Session minutes, fell by about a quarter and stayed low throughout the 1850s until the death of the Rev John Eadie in 1857. The religious census of 1851, albeit generally regarded as not very reliable, gives one third of the population attending morning service in Scotland so Dun's attendance may still have been above average. Under John Eadie's successor, Charles McLean, numbers rose steadily, following the trend throughout the country. The naming of regular communicants was not continued after the Disruption, so the church-going habits of the Burnsiders are unknown.

Intelligent young working class men in the first half of the 19th century often toured the different Presbyterian churches, "tasting" theological varieties. John Stool, who came from a dissenting family – his father had been a deacon of the Berean Church at Sauchieburn and attended the Secession Church in Brechin – joined the Established Church briefly as a young man in 1813 "according to the custom of the country, but Mr Waugh, Menmuir, dwelt so much on vowing that I withdrew [in] 1816". Most of his life though he seems to have followed the family tradition of worshipping at the Berean[7] meeting house at Sauchieburn where he met his wife, and where his sister Elizabeth may also have met her husband, the shoemaker from St Cyrus, James Moir.

There were no dissenting churches or meeting places in the parish although many in Brechin and Montrose, especially the former. The *Angus and Mearns Directory* for 1846, published three years after the Disruption, lists dissenting congregations, including the new Free Churches, in both these towns and in Edzell, Maryton and Logie and of course Sauchieburn. Country people, as we have noted, were used to covering long distances on foot in those days and Brechin, four to five miles away along the cattle raik, would have been a reasonable distance away for a Sunday service. That country-dwellers could be deeply involved in town dissenting meetings is demonstrated by Joseph Petrie, a weaver in Leys of Dun in the late 18th century. He appears as Manager of the Congregation in the records of the Associate Congregation of Brechin (Anti-Burghers), which was established in 1768 as an off-shoot of the Montrose church[8]. As such he helped to run the finances and fabric of the establishment in City Road, Brechin. In the OPR Joseph Petrie's residences are given as Balnillie and Cottertown of Balnillie, the probable precursor of Burnside. The meetings of Managers were fairly frequent and he did not miss many. Nevertheless, sectarianism does not seem to have discouraged baptism or marriage in the Established Church. In the late 1700s, three of Joseph Petrie's sons were baptised and one buried by the Minister of Dun. All of Elizabeth and James Moir's children, baptised in the Berean chapel at Sauchieburn, were entered into the baptismal register in Dun. Only a single Burnside marriage recorded in the post-1855 Statutory Register was solemnised by a non-Established minister.

Under the Old Poor Law of Scotland (notably the Act of 1672) it was the Church that was responsible for poor relief, through the offices of the Kirk Elders. The Parish of Dun raised funds for the poor through voluntary assessment – that is from collections at the Sunday services or from door-to-door efforts. In addition, funds came from the rent of the parish mortcloth at funerals, bequests (mortifications), gifts from individuals and special collections, for example at the annual Communion Sunday service in July.

The Old Poor Law legislation identified four classes of the poor, only one of which was entitled to regular parochial relief: children, the old and the disabled. These were the "ordinary poor". The "occasional poor" had no legal right to relief, but were usually supported. John Eadie reported to the Royal Commission on the Old Poor Law that 37 paupers were relieved in 1842 with a total of £49 9s 3d, the elderly receiving 4s. per month and a few families receiving more, according to their size. Such a high number of paupers was unusual and reflects the exceptionally hard times of the early 1840s.

The New Poor Law of 1845 had little effect on the lives of the poor themselves. Assessment remained voluntary in Dun. In Scotland there were far fewer people on poor rolls than in England and the amount spent on them one-third to a half less per head. The Heritors' Minutes for 1845 and 1846 lists the "Poor belonging to the Parish who receive Aliment monthly and occasionally from the Poors Fund". Nine paupers in the parish and eight living out of the parish received regular relief (amounting to a total of £4 18s 0d per month) ranging from 4s to 15s per person, while three others were relieved occasionally. In 1841 Burnside accounted for 10% of the population of Dun yet around half (five out of nine) of the paupers in the parish lived there. The Burnside paupers were Widow Kandow, Widow Moir, at that time with three children under 13, Widow Ford with two children, Francis Fraser (who died in 1846 at the age of 46) and Robert Smith the weaver and elder, then aged 80. This worthy received 4s per month at a time when labourers were earning around 2s a day. In winter, paupers might also be given coals.

The Poor records for Dun have been lost, but more than 40 years later the Parochial Board was dealing with a similar number of paupers. In 1889, seven paupers received between 2s 6d and 6s 6d per week. None of these lived in Burnside, as far as can be ascertained, but over the next few years three old people in Burnside applied for relief. In 1894, Ann Burnett applied but was not considered "a proper subject for relief", perhaps because she lived with her son Peter, then in his forties and working as an agricultural labourer.[9] A year later, the new Parish Council considered the case of Peter Connar and his wife, both paupers and both "in a feeble state" in their early 60s. The Medical Officer advised their removal to the Poorhouse in Forfar or the provision of someone to look after them. Poorhouses in Scotland were not the same as workhouses in England. Originally they were provided for those who had no-one to look after them at home (the helpless), although later unmarried mothers and other groups deemed idle or immoral were sent there. The Parochial Board decided on the Poorhouse but added "in the event of his refusing, his allowance was not to be stopped, and he was to get a load of Coals to put him over the winter."[10] The Board minutes show that the couple did go to the poorhouse, where Peter soon died. Another old man died before he reached the poorhouse – George Menmuir, the Church Officer or Beadle leaving a widow, Ann, who was granted 4s a week. She was then aged 85. The Council then spent some time and effort trying to extract a refund of this relief from her son who lived in St Cyrus, but without success. Paupers with relations who could support them had always been either denied relief or loaned money and not placed on the roll: the burden of caring for the poor usually rested on the poor. Ann Menmuir died in 1905 in Burnside at the age of 90. She may be the old woman in Jane Ann Duthie's essay on Burnside.

Until 1873, the kirk's main responsibility was education and there had always been a parochial school in Dun. The school is not mentioned in the OSA but in the neighbouring parish of Logie Pert the quarterly fee paid by the scholars for reading in the 1790s was 1s 6d and for writing 2s. 3s 6d then was the equivalent of around 8 days' work for a day labourer. It was common for poorer children to go to school in the winter months only and from the age of seven or eight to be employed in the summer. Nevertheless, if we are to believe the Rev John Eadie's report in the New Statistical Account of 1833, "there are no person above six years of age who cannot either read or write". In 1843, John Eadie reported to the Royal Commission on the Poor Law (Scotland) that only two or three children came from families which could not afford to pay the school fees and that Kirk Session funds and special collections paid for three or four years of the Three Rs for these poor children. The statutory registers of births, marriages and deaths which start in 1855 reveal only the very occasional cross of an illiterate person. Brechin Presbytery examined the school in 1859 and described the scholars as a "respectable class of children … [although] ... not expert in their exercises"[11] perhaps because the schoolteacher was getting old, or because of irregular attendance.

In 1873 following the passing of the Education Act (Scotland), the newly elected School Board carried out a census of all children of school age in the parish. They found that there were 114 children between the ages of five and thirteen, of whom 93 (82%) were attending school. The school attendance registers have not survived, but the log book, kept by Robert Spalding, schoolteacher, Kirk Session Clerk, Census Enumerator and School Board Secretary from 1873 until his death in 1892 has, and it tells an almost unchanging story, year after year, of the seasonal catastrophes that closed the school: snow in the winter, epidemics in the early spring and – most disruptive of all – the harvest and the tattie-howking in the autumn. The school year began in February, which was often the height of the epidemic season. New children arrived in June, just after the Whitsun feeing fairs, when families were moving in and fathers starting new jobs. Until 1891 the summer holiday began in the middle of August – around harvest time – and classes resumed in the middle of September. Although the Scottish Education Act of 1873 had made elementary education compulsory, attendance fluctuated wildly. October and November were the worst months: on 6 November 1875, "numbers gradually increasing; upwards of one half of the children between 5 and 13 years of age still absent". In 1882 the log for 27 October irritably reports: "Attendance very thin – upwards of one half of the scholars absent – a few employed lifting potatoes but the greater part loitering about at home". In 1889, 80% of the children – mainly the older pupils – were absent in early October, this figure falling to 36% a month later. We may guess that there was some tension between the schoolmaster and the School Board over attendance: in at least one year (1879) the Board suspended compulsory attendance so that the children could work at the potato harvest and in 1893, it declared a three week holiday for tattie-howking. Winter meant infectious diseases: "school nearly deserted, scarlatina [scarlet fever] having broken out in the Parish" reads the entry for 29 January 1875. The epidemic affected attendance until the end of February, then at the end of April "about one-third of the children absent from school, being employed planting potatoes".

The School Inspector on his annual visits generally found Dun School well run. The 1878 report, summarised in the School Log, noted that "discipline is satisfactory" and "a good pass is made in Standard Subjects" although "a little more energy is wanted" in the Infants where the teacher was Robert Spalding's sister Mary.

Until their abolition in 1890, school fees were set by the Board. In 1871, parents paid 2s 6d per quarter for infants, rising to 4s 6d per quarter for the top class. Latin, Maths and Book-keeping were extra. In 1874, the Board ruled that no more than two and a half children per family should pay fees. Pupils also paid 6d per quarter coal money during the winter.

As the school registers have not survived, we do not know how the Burnside children compared with other parish children in attendance. We may guess that they were poorer than average, and so may have been amongst the 21 not attending school in 1873. The only time a family is mentioned in the School Board minutes is in 1894: "the Clerk was instructed to intimate to David Croall, residing at Burnside, that his children were not in a fit state to attend school, and ask him to have this rectified before the school meets after the holiday."

The kirk oversaw public morality. Earlier in the century the Kirk Session was satisfied that drunkenness was not a problem in Dun. In a letter addressed to the General Assembly's Committee for the Suppression of Intemperance, copied into the Kirk Session Minutes for November 1848, John Eadie, wrote that "the farming population is sober and industrious." Moreover "[t]here is no public house in the Parish except a Toll house near one boundary of it and it is not known to be frequented by the Parishioners. There is no class of the population particularly addicted to Intemperance. There seems to be no excess at private baptisms, Marriages or Funerals etc…Any changes that may have taken place in the Parish may be said to be for the better from a small public House being abolished." Therefore, the letter concludes, there is no need for "direct interference" as recommended by the Suppression of Intemperance Committee. The Elders and the Minister were mainly concerned with the habits of the poor and the conclusions of the Report by the Committee, published in 1849, were that drunkenness in Scotland was entirely a product of the existence of public houses. It is hard to imagine that the Elders of the Parish would have been much concerned about drinking at – say – House of Dun, where in 1809–10 (admittedly a more relaxed age), the laird spent £40 10s 9½d on rum, sherry and "bottles"[12] at a time when day labourers' wages were 8d or 9d a day.

In the second half of the century, as we have seen, the shebeen in the hamlet was well patronised at least by the unmarried ploughmen of the area. The drove road and the market stance would also have kept a small tavern in business at this strategic point. We do not know whether this caused a drink problem either for the parish or the hamlet. But, as the following chapter will tell, the Kirk Session did not overtly police drinking, its time being almost wholly taken up with another moral issue – antenuptial fornication.

From the fragments of documentary evidence described in this chapter, we cannot do more than guess at the depth of the influence of the landowners and the kirk on the poor of the parish. Only the extent of illegitimacy hints at a "counterculture" these interests could not reach.

NOTES

[1]   Jacob, *op cit*, p. 291.

[2]   A Carnegy rental document for 1844 shows that Balwyllo and Balnillo yielded £1058.16.2. Carnegy of Craigo papers, NLS, Dep 267: 91.

[3]   M. A. Crowther, Poverty, Wealth and Welfare, in W.H. Fraser and R.J. Morris *People and Society in Scotland II 1830-1914*, Edinburgh 1990, p. 265.

[4]   Dun School Board Minute Book, 1873-1909, Angus Archives ACC6/75/1/1.

[5]   T.C. Smout, *A Century of the Scottish People 1830-1950*, London 1986, p.183.

[6]   J. A. Duthie, Diary 1896-1915, Angus Archives MS 610.

[7]   The Berean church was founded in 1773 in Edinburgh by a former Church of Scotland minister, John Barclay. Most adherents joined the Congregationalists after Barclay's death. The name Bereans came from the biblical Bereans of Acts xvii. 11 who studied scripture as a guide to daily life.

[8]   United Presbyterian Church, City Road, Brechin, Angus Archives MS414/20.

[9]   Dun Parochial Board Minute Book, 1889-1923, Angus Archives ACC9/12/1/1.

[10]   Ibid.

[11]   J. C. Jessop, *Education in Angus*, London 1931, p. 141.

[12]   Dun Estate papers, NAS, GD123/463.

Chapter Seven

Illegitimacy

"the scandal of her sin"

"To be hoped on the decrease" was the Minister of Dun's response in 1843 to the question from the Royal Commission on the Poor Law: "Is bastardy on the increase, or on the decrease, amongst the labouring classes in your parish?"[1]. The Old Parochial Records (OPR) and Kirk Session minutes record some children born out of wedlock in Dun before the 1850s but the Statutory Registers of Births reveal a staggeringly high proportion of illegitimate births in Burnside itself, from 1855 on. John Eadie's hope was pious indeed.

The great divide in Victorian sexual attitudes was not only the now well known chasm between the prudishness of public middle class morality (and the ignorance of middle class girls in particular) and the behaviour of many middle class husbands, sons and brothers. There was also a gulf between the behaviour and attitudes of the urban and the rural working classes. Illegitimate births were higher in rural areas than in the cities although there were huge variations across Scotland. Flinn[2] and Smout[3] have shown that these were not directly connected to rates of illiteracy, churchgoing, drunkenness, the bothy system or overcrowding, but to economic and specifically, employment differences and courtship patterns. Smout argues that in the Highlands, where illegitimate births were much rarer, and where girls lived and worked on the family croft and had no income independent of their families, parental control was strict and the tradition of "bundling" – couples sleeping in the same bed before marriage – was accepted because it usually did not involve sex. It was the rural counties of the Lowlands that saw the highest numbers of illegitimate births in the second half of the 19th century. In farming districts, girls could find year-round paid and residential employment, away from the family home. Banffshire, for example had the highest proportion of illegitimate births in Scotland in the 1850s: 16% of live births. Parishes in this county have been studied by Andrew Blaikie[4] and although there are significant differences between his parish of Rothiemay in Banffshire and that of Dun, in particular the crofting economy in the former, his investigation and conclusions shed much light on what was going on in Burnside. In both Angus and the North East girls who fell pregnant would have been able to have the child cared for by their mothers, and so to return to work, paying part of their wages to them. Like other farm servants or agricultural labourers, girls were used to moving from job to job very frequently, so were relatively free from parental (or neighbourly) oversight from an early age. To the frequent despair of ministers, doctors and other commentators, mistresses rarely exerted moral control over their servants.

Angus, a prosperous farming county with large farms employing many unmarried farm servants, had precisely the right conditions for a high rate of illegitimacy. And in fact, the illegitimacy ratio (number of illegitimate births per 100 live births) throughout the second half of the 19th century was well above the national average, placing Angus in eighth place in the league table.

	1855–60	1861–5	1866–70	1871–5	1876–80	1881–5	1886–90
Angus	10.67	12.43	11.63	10.47	10.13	9.96	9.84
Scotland	8.74	9.79	9.85	09	8.49	8.27	8.04

Source: Flinn (1977) Table 5.4.1

Table 7.1 Illegitimacy ratios in Scotland and Angus, 1855–1890

But the illegitimacy ratio in Burnside far outstripped that of Angus. Between 1855 and 1887, when the last child was born in Burnside, of 51 live births, 15 were illegitimate. In the parish as a whole, there were 64 illegitimate births out of a total of 564 live births and in the neighbouring parish of Maryton the figures were 62 out of 423 . With such small numbers, percentages can be misleading, but it is worth noting that as a proportion of live births, illegitimate births in Burnside were nearly three times the proportion in the whole parish. All the unmarried mothers in Burnside were domestic servants or farm labourers, but for one linen bleacher. All had families living in Burnside. Their average age, at the birth of their first child, was 21 years – the age range was from 19 to 28.

In Burnside, "antenuptial fornication" often, as elsewhere in Scotland, ran in families although not perhaps to the extent of Peter Laslett's "bastardy prone sub society" where giving birth outside wedlock becomes a cultural tradition handed on from mother to daughter through the generations[5]. Three Candy sisters, whose widowed mother had appeared before the Kirk Session in 1846 charged with fornication with a married man, had seven illegitimate children amongst them between 1856 and 1868. Their mother may have been the Ann Kandow who registered the births of a son and twins by different fathers in the 1830s in the OPR. The agricultural labourer Ann Simpson was living in Burnside in 1861. She had two illegitimate sons born of different fathers in Fearn and Montrose. Ten years later her illegitimate niece, Mary Davidson, then living with her, had a daughter born out of wedlock, named Agnes Croll McFarlane Davidson. The Smith sisters Christina and Helen, daughters of Christina Smith or Lindsay, a widow, each gave birth to an illegitimate child in the 1850s. One of Elizabeth Stool's daughters – Elizabeth Moir – and her granddaughter Elizabeth Young were unmarried mothers. Jane Shepherd, the illegitimate daughter of Elisabeth Soutar had her own illegitimate child in 1870 with George Kenny. As this was a "trilapse case … in so far as it relates to the said George Kenny", the Kirk Session referred it to the Presbytery of Brechin.

It would appear that there was no question of unmarried mothers being sent away from the family to conceal their shame. On the contrary, census enumeration books show several living with their parents or aunts. In many cases it was one of these relatives who registered the birth: baby Agnes Davidson's birth was registered by her mother's cousin (Mary Ann died of puerperal fever three days after the birth). Elizabeth Moir's son-in-law James Smith (and James C Smith's father) registered the births of his two illegitimate great nephews by marriage. Grandparents and other family members helped to raise the children too: six illegitimate children (not all born there) were living with relatives in the hamlet in 1871, out of a total of twenty-two children under the age of fifteen. These relatives were not only grandparents, but mothers, uncles, aunts and stepfathers. Jane Shepherd for example lived with her mother, her mother's husband and their young family. The Dun Poor Records have been lost but there is no indication in the census returns that any unmarried mothers were in receipt of poor relief, although it is unlikely that they would have qualified. Rev John Eadie's response to the Royal Commission's question on whether relief was given to unmarried mothers was "Rarely", while the Minister of Craig (Ferryden)'s reply by contrast was "Yes and they are often the heaviest burden."[6]

We can, then, as Andrew Blaikie's account suggests, picture daughters in domestic or farm service around the county returning home to their parents when they fall pregnant, and then leaving their children with them as they go off again to find work. The high proportion of such children in Burnside is not therefore a consequence of loose living in the hamlet but a "registration effect". It may be that the conditions of service also encouraged repeat "offences" such as Ann Simpson's.

Illegitimacy was not outlawed by the community in Lowland Scotland. Government investigators in the 1860s "noted the absence of any stigma on a girl who lost her virginity before marriage, or even on a woman who had borne a bastard: abortion and infanticide were not practised as there was 'no pressure on the woman to commit any crime' and, among her own class, 'no feeling of indignation aroused in consequence of what they would call her "misfortune"'"[7]. Smout quotes W. Cramond's 1888 study *Illegitimacy in Banffshire: facts, figures and opinions*: "the only thing they seem to feel is if the father does not acknowledge the child. A woman who had five illegitimate children said to me that her mother said she was just the one to have them, as she always got a father."[8] We do not always know the fathers, but those who are named were all working on farms outwith the parish. The father of Jessie Smith's child lived at Easter Memus, the other side of Brechin; the father of Helen Smith's son lived in Fordoun before absconding to America; Margaret Candy told the Kirk Session that Joseph McHardy, "an unmarried man residing at Smallbank in the Parish of Marykirk had been guilty with her and was the father of her twin children". Joseph thereafter wrote to the elders acknowledging his offspring. Not many, if any, subsequently married the fathers, as far as can be ascertained, and most seem to have remained unmarried. We find Christina Smith (the younger) for example aged 48, employed at Balwyllo in 1881 as a "domestic servant General" and living on her own in Balwyllo Cottage. Elizabeth Moir junior, the mother of James McNab who emigrated to Australia and, with his cousin James C. Smith, erected the memorial in Burnside in 1930, worked as a nurse in Edinburgh and in England and never married[9]. Two mothers, Isabella Candy and the widow Jessie Smith subsequently married men (both ploughmen, the aristocrats of the farm workforce) who were not the fathers of their illegitimate offspring.

But the Church and its supporters took illegitimacy extremely seriously.

After 1858 when the Fourth Annual Report of the Register General for Scotland published county illegitimacy totals which dramatically revealed the full extent of bastardy amongst farm workers, an outraged and anguished debate took place amongst the clergy and other commentators. Bothies and the shortage of housing for farm servants were held mainly responsible, although hiring fairs, the employment of young women and even oatmeal had their supporters. There followed a series of attempts to improve the situation through education and moral crusades.

In Dun, until the 1880s when financial and building issues started to occupy the elders' minds rather more, the Kirk Session met almost exclusively to consider cases of fornication. Meetings were held four or five times a year and at nearly every one an unmarried mother – and the very occasional man – was present, either to be accused or to be admonished after confession. Until the woman and, if possible, the child's father, had appeared before the Kirk Session three times at fortnightly intervals to acknowledge their guilt, been admonished and finally received absolution of their sin, the child could not be baptised.

It is difficult, in the absence of the testimony of the mothers or their families, to measure how embarrassing and painful this process was. It no longer took place in front of the whole congregation or on a stool of repentance as previously, but more privately in the school house or the kirk. It was the elders' responsibility to patrol the parish and so to report on immorality (and on applicants for poor relief too). However, the policing of parish morals does seem also to have been a means of ensuring that the father paid something – aliment – towards the upkeep of the child. In a few cases indeed the man named as the father denied his guilt, but still agreed to sponsor the child.

Very few men appeared before Dun Kirk Session side by side with an unmarried mother. In the 1850s, in swift succession, the two daughters of Christina Smith, Christina and Helen Smith, both handloom weavers, were charged with fornication. The matter of Christina's guilt and absolution took three years to resolve, one cause of delay being the father's reluctance to have anything to do with the child's baptism as he was a member of the Free Church. Helen's case lasted almost as long. The Kirk Session took considerable pains to track down the father, writing to the Kirk Session of Fordoun only to find he had left his place. Helen Smith too "stated that she and her friends had done everything in their power to discover his place of abode, and that they at last found that he had gone to America. "Taking into consideration the long delay in this case and being satisfied that she was conducting herself in a becoming manner and seemed penitent" the Session "resolved to admit her to discipline. She was therefore solemnly exhorted to repentance … and allowed to have the child baptised."[10] In the 1861 census, both these boys, James Irons and John Campbell, are recorded as living in Burnside with their mothers and grandmother – although they are not described as illegitimate, unlike the two sons of Ann Simpson, a 30-year-old agricultural labourer recently moved from Brechin. Ann had also appeared before Dun Kirk Session, in 1859, soon after the birth of her younger son. She accused Alexander Christie of fathering the boy and as he denied it, she was obliged to give details. "She stated that he had connection with her in the Barn at Balwyllo and also among the hay when putting it into ricks in the field and that Charles Smith the foreman saw them."[11] Christie stuck to his guns. Unusually, this case faded away. But the child is recorded in the 1861 Census as John Christie.

By no means all the illegitimate births recorded in the statutory registers were dealt with by the Kirk Session (and the elders never heard cases of fornication which did not result in a child). The Session process itself also gradually seems to have become shorter and somewhat less severe. In the 1871 census, Jessie Smith appears as a widow living with her elderly parents, John and Margaret Watt, her two legitimate children and an illegitimate one-year old daughter Mary Ann, all the children bearing the surname Smith. Jessie "compeared" before the Session in October 1870 "confessing she had been guilty of fornication". For the first time, the Minister and elders took a more lenient approach. "From their knowledge of the whole circumstances of the case the Session declined to cite the said James Burnett [accused as Mary Ann's father by Jessie] and the Moderator having seriously rebuked and solemnly admonished the said Jessie Smith … absolved her from the scandal of her sin and restored her to the privileges of the Church."[12] The following month Jane Shepherd's case seems to have been dealt with in one rather than three meetings. Nevertheless Dun Kirk Session continued to deal with cases of fornication into the 20th century.

T.C. Smout in *A Century of the Scottish People* has argued that parental control of courting was much laxer in working class families than in the middle classes, especially in the countryside. Couples could spend hours together alone after dark behind a haystack or in a barn without falling foul of parents' wrath. These meetings did not always lead to sexual intercourse – Smout describes them as "heavy petting"[13].

Andrew Blaikie argues convincingly that there was "a graduated process where women married soon after conceiving when nuptial opportunities were favourable, delayed marriage when chances were more constrained, and bore illegitimates when these were slightest"[14] and that it was very often the availability or otherwise of housing that determined whether or not a couple married. In addition, and this is particularly relevant to Burnside, geographical mobility and the expansion of agricultural service provided more chances for casual sexual encounters, after which the man could move on to another farm (and disappear).

We end with a puzzle. In 1823, the OPR records that Magdalene Cruikshank in Burnside gave birth to a natural son, Alexander Law, whose father, also Alexander, was from Montrose. Magdalene Cruikshank erected a gravestone in Old Dun churchyard in memory of this son, who died aged 23 in 1845. The stone also records her own death in 1875 at the age of 82, apparently still unmarried. It is more than likely that Homer Cruikshank added the inscription for his older sister, but perhaps this stone tells us that her sin was regarded as of so little account that it could be made public in the kirkyard.

NOTES

[1]   Poor Law Inquiry Commission for Scotland, Appendix V.

[2]   Flinn (ed), *op cit*, p. 356

[3]   Smout, *op cit*, p.166.

[4]   A Blaikie, *Illegitimacy, Sex and Society – North-East Scotland 1750–1900*, Oxford 1993.

[5]   P. Laslett and K Oosterveen (1973) Long term trends in bastardy in England *Population Studies*, Vol 27, 1973, pp 255–86.

[6]   Poor Law Inquiry Commission for Scotland, Appendix V.

[7]   Smout, *op cit* page 167.

[8]   Ibid, page 168.

[9]   Personal communication from Robyn Hukin.

[10] Dun Kirk Session Minutes 27 June 1858. National Records of Scotland CH2/1022/1.

[11] Ibid, 17 July 1859.

[12] Ibid, 16 October 1870.

[13] Smout, *op cit*, p. 169

[14] Blaikie *op cit*, p. 217.

Chapter Eight

Desertion

"and the hooses were alooed to gae to pieces"

There's naething left to mark the place
But ae hoose on Dunside
And the bonnie burnie rinnin' past
The dear auld Burnside
Elizabeth Moir

In May 1930, James Cruikshank Smith and his cousin James McNab erected a small Celtic cross on the site of their grandmother's house beside the drove road. The monument "marks the site of one of the houses which formed a tiny group in that sequestered spot in Angus" reported the *Montrose Review*, which also informed its readers that "(t)he monument has a somewhat romantic origin. Its inscription tells its own story and reads:

> Erected by James McNab and J.C. Smith on the site of the house where they were born in memory of their grandparents, James Moir and Elizabeth Stool, who lived and died here; their mothers, Isabella and Elizabeth Moir, who were brought up here, and all their good friends and neighbours in the vanished hamlet of Burnside."[1]

Andrew Lamb, once gardener but now "overseer" on the Dun Estate told the *Review* that "as one by one [the houses] dropped out of habitation they fell into decay and gradually disappeared"[2]. By 1930, only what was known as the Beadle's Cottage still stood.

When did Burnside become depopulated, and why? In 1891, the

census enumeration book lists eighteen inhabitants and seven households in Burnside of Balnillo and Burnside of Dun. The 1901 Census does not name the settlement: the elderly Beadle, George Menmuir, whose address had been Burnside of Dun ten years earlier, is recorded as living in Leys of Dun Cottage. Elizabeth Milne, the School dinner lady, also listed as a Burnsider in 1891, was living at Woodside Balnillo, which appears on the Third edition OS map, published in 1908, about half a mile from the hamlet. This map shows the Beadle's house and the house at the western end of the site (labelled House F on the sketchmap). On the other hand, other records such as the Parish Council minutes and gravestones mention Burnside well into the 20th century.

There may be little mystery as to why people should have decided to leave the small, crudely-built and probably decaying houses with earthen floors and turf roofs, straggling alongside the drove road, now scarcely used since the end of cattle droving in the 1880s. There were fewer farm jobs than there had been and fewer apprenticeships in rural trades, and far more opportunities for better paid and pleasanter work in Brechin and Montrose, to say nothing of Dundee and further afield.

The decline in agricultural employment in the UK as a whole set in with the agricultural depression of the 1870s. However, the mixed farming of the east of Scotland largely escaped the worst effects of the depression, and of the fall in grain prices caused by North American imports. But the move towards stock-breeding that the depression encouraged meant fewer hands were needed for harvest, and also that fewer specialised workers, especially ploughmen, were needed. Mechanisation too reduced the demand for both skilled farm servants and general labourers[3].

As the economic value of a settlement of unskilled labourers to the local farmers was disappearing, casual work dried up. At the same time, the growth of better paid jobs in pleasanter conditions in towns particularly in the service sector was, as we have noted above (see Chapter 3) attracting country people. It is a moot point whether rural depopulation was a result of the draw of the towns or the decline in agricultural employment, or both, possibly at different stages.

The part-time or seasonal work offered by handloom weaving had virtually disappeared in the countryside by the end of the century and droving too. The viability of Burnside as a self-sufficient settlement was clearly in question.

The living conditions in the hamlet were probably worsening, both absolutely as the population dwindled and aged, and by comparison with other villages. Apart from the state of the clay-built houses themselves, which needed careful maintenance to remain watertight, the lack of proper drains and waste disposal must have contributed to unpleasant as well as unhealthy conditions.

From the sparse documentary evidence, the impression is that by the 1890s, Burnside had become something of a rural slum, inhabited by the elderly and to some extent by transient people. No-one who appeared in the 1891 census had lived there for twenty years, unlike previous censuses (see Table 3.2). The case of the labourer David Croll or Croall may be instructive. We know from the official records that over his lifetime of 69 years, from 1851 to 1920, he lived in seven different places in Kincardine and North Angus, and there are many large gaps in this timeline. His three children were born in Brechin and Arbuthnott (Kincardineshire). The Schoolmaster of Dun noted that when they enrolled in the summer of 1894 "neither of [the older children, then aged nine and twelve] knew the letters of the alphabet"[4]. This may have been the result of frequent flittings by the family.

The age structure changed radically: in the Censuses of 1871 and 1881, the over 60s accounted for less than 1.5% of the total population (seven out of 49 and two out of 26 respectively); in 1891, six out of seventeen inhabitants (around one third) were over 60.

Searches of census records and the Registers of Birth, Marriages and Deaths have failed to track down many of those who left Burnside. Of the Pender family – ten children, their Irish father and their Aberdeenshire mother – no trace remains after the 1881 Census. The large family tombstone in the new graveyard in Dun bears the name of a single child, Andrew, who died aged three, of scarlatina, in 1877. It is conceivable that they emigrated, like several of the Muir family. The Smiths (Elizabeth's daughter Isobella and her second husband James Smith) moved to Tayock, just outside Montrose and on or near the main road to Brechin, so presumably much more conveniently placed for work and for the Academy, where James C. Smith was a pupil.

The only families in the parish who were severely criticised for poor hygiene in the extant Parochial Board and Council and School Board minutes lived in Burnside. In 1890 the Parochial Board instructed the Public Health Inspector to "take the necessary steps to cause [Mary Ann Cuthill or

Maclaggan] to get her house and family properly cleaned, both at present being in a most filthy state"[5]. The School Board, as mentioned above, chastised another family, the Croalls, for sending the children to school in an unfit state. The few people still living in the hamlet later in the decade included several paupers, a financial burden which weighed heavily on the Parish Council: one applicant was refused relief and two others were sent to the poorhouse in Forfar.

Jane Anne Duthie writing in 1912 recalls a familiar tale of death and migration:

> Some of the auld tenants dee'd and the hooses were alooed to gae to pieces; ithers left and gaed to toons to end their days in garrets, etc., as their hooses gaed dune afore them.[6]

So the hamlet seems to have died a natural death, without evictions or the sudden closing down of a source of employment. Whether other settlements in Angus, or the Eastern Lowlands, suffered a similar fate at this period is not known, with the exception of Pitmiddle, in the eastern Sidlaws. Pitmiddle was a large village which started to become depopulated in the first half of the 19th century – when Burnside was burgeoning. In 1841, there were 99 inhabitants and by 1891, only five. Although Pitmiddle had a different life story, having become a village of pendiclers after the best arable land was enclosed and amalgamated in the previous century, it seems likely that similar factors led to its demise – remoteness from modern means of communication and the increasing difficulty of making a living from a small patch of land and casual labouring. One difference however is that the houses, which had been of clay, were rebuilt with stone as early as the 1820s[7].

When the present author began to inquire about Burnside of Dun in 1977, two retired farmers living in Montrose who remembered the place were interviewed. Mr James Couper, born in 1908, farmed North Mains of Dun and looked after the memorial. He recalled a family of drainers who lived there, and the beadles who had the cottage until it was sold to become a holiday house after the Second World War. Mr Ewan, born about the same time, farmed Muirton of Ballochy till 1963. His father was the blacksmith and was at school with J.C. Smith, and told his son about the tailor, the shoemaker and the "Jeanie a'thing" who lived in Burnside. As a boy, Mr Ewan picked apples and pears at the deserted hamlet and saw the clay walls still standing.

Mr A Knox of Dundee wrote to the *Courier* in 1977, in response to a plea for memories of Burnside, about "playing around there with my school pals in the 1920s … It was already a ruin and seemed to have been that way for many years. It was overgrown with bushes, fruit trees, raspberries etc."

Burnside of Dun earns no mention in either the Old or the New Statistical Account. The only 19th-century published reference mention of Burnside as a settlement is in John Bartholomew's *Gazetteer of the British Isles of 1887* which describes the parish of Dun as follows:

> Dun, par. (ry. sta. Bridge of Dun, 5¾ miles W. of Montrose; P.O.), NE. Forfarshire, 4306 ac., pop. 541; contains Dun House, seat, Dun's Dish, loch, and the hamlets of Burnside of Dun and Muir of Dun.[8]

The Account of Dun for the *Third Statistical Account*, written in 1951 and revised in 1967 does grant it a brief description, under the subheading "Ancient Drove Road". It is worth quoting in full as it may be the origin of some of the current myths about the hamlet:

> The lowest of the fields on the west side of the farm of North Mains of Dun is called the Market Muir. It is on the site of the original Dun Cattle Market. Just south of it runs the old cattle rake or 'drove road'. This is a most interesting ancient highway, and remnants can yet be traced in the parishes of Kinneff, Bervie, Garvock, Logie Pert and Dun. It was down this road that the cattle from the north-east made their way to 'Taranty Tryst' near Brechin, at one time among the most important stock sales in Scotland, and still farther south to the famous Falkirk Tryst. At the other side of the cattle rake was the site of the now vanished village of Burnside. There is only one house remaining where there used to be 'forty reeking lums'. Tradition claims it to have been a weavers' village and to have contained a shebeen or ale-house. A fine granite monument has been erected by two cousins James McNab and J.C. Smith who were born in the village. J.C. Smith, educated in the Dun school when one dominie looked after 90 children in one dimly lit room, rose to be Chief Inspector of schools in Scotland. On his death in 1947 this monument was handed over to the Kirk Session with a small endowment to keep it in repair.[9]

As I have shown, the documentary evidence is clear: there were never more than 18 households (with a lum apiece presumably) and the weavers were a minority of the working population. Most of this paragraph from the Third Statistical Account closely resembles material in an article about North Mains of Dun published in the *Montrose Standard* by "Lea Rig". The "forty reeking lums" story is credited in this article to Mr James Couper's father who would have known the hamlet when it was at its most flourishing in the 1860s.[10]

Deserted villages have a romantic melancholy about them, especially when there are living memories. Most of Burnside of Dun has never been cleared or ploughed up and although there is some recent planting near the burn, the place seems little changed since it was last inhabited, around 120 years ago.

A row of mature beeches stands behind the first cottage on the drove road and there are other large beeches in the same places as trees marked on the First edition OS map. Gooseberry bushes still flourish by the remains of three of the cottages. The marshy area in the centre of the site probably attests to broken wells and drains (several wells are marked on the First edition map). Apple and pear trees can live to over 100 years, but there is no sign of them today. Hawthorns and gean now blossom in early summer in their place. Across the cattle raik are gorse and whins, as there were long ago, although they are now confined to a narrow field margin. Small birds, hare, roe deer and possibly badgers are the 21st century inhabitants, along with the pheasants fed there; now that the cattle raik leads nowhere, few people pass.

At the beginning of our period, Sir David Wilkie achieved national fame with his painting of a village in Fife, *Pitlessie Fair* (1804). In this picture, Wilkie presents, with humour but also realistically, 'a portrait of a village and its people'[11]. 140 recognisable people are portrayed haggling, drinking, quarrelling, laughing, thieving. Gradually through the 19th century, the educated gaze withdrew further and further from the living reality of the village, preferring views of '[r]uined people to set beside decayed buildings.'[12] This is the spirit of Wordsworth's poem *The Deserted Cottage* (see Introduction). Burnside was relatively removed from the daily oversight of the minister, the schoolmaster and the farmers. There is something complacent about John Eadie's statement in the New Statistical Account that there was no village in the parish. Villages were certainly suspected in some quarters of being nests of immorality and the evidence of high rates of illegitimacy in Burnside, while not suggesting it was a lair of outlaws (witness the church-going) tend to support an impression of a place apart.

It may be that this is why Burnside has been more written about and remembered as a melancholy ruin than as a noisy, tumbledown, dirty and smelly daily reality.

NOTES

[1]   *The Montrose Review*, 2 May 1930.

[2]   Ibid.

[3]   M. Gray, Farm workers in North East Scotland. In T.M. Devine (ed), *Farm Servants and Labour in Lowland Scotland 1770–1914*, John Donald, Edinburgh 1984.

[4]   Dun School Log 25/6/1894, Angus Archives, ACC 6

[5]   Dun Parochial Board Minutes, 1889–1923, Angus Archives, ACC 9/12/1/1

[6]   Duthie, *op cit*, p. 122.

[7]   Abernyte website (no date) *Pitmiddle – a short history*. Available at http://www.abernyte. org/pitmiddle, date accessed:18/11/2013.

[8]   J. Bartholomew, *Gazetteer of the British Isles*, 1887, GB Historical GIS / University of Portsmouth, History of Dun in Angus | Map and description, *A Vision of Britain through Time*. URL: http://www.visionofbritain.org.uk/place/16765, date accessed: 13/5/2013.

[9]   Account of Dun, County of Angus, 3rd Statistical Account of Scotland, Edinburgh, 1977.

[10]   *Montrose Standard*, 8 June 1950.

[11]   P. Cunningham, *Life of Sir David Wilkie* vol 1 p.164, cited in J. Morrison, *Painting the Nation* Edinburgh 2003.

[12]   Morrison, *op cit*, p.101.

Epilogue

The Auld Burnside, Parish of Dun, near Montrose

I see again my Mither's hoose
And clean white-washed fireside
For all I ever kent o' hame
Was at the Burnside.

I see auld Homer noddin' past
His pirn creel by his side
For loom and shuttle ance went fast
About the Burnside
But whaur are a' the weavers noo
Wha worked the hale day lang:
The beam and shuttle blithely drew
Wi' mony a joke and sang?

And whaur are a' the laddies noo –
They're scattered far and wide
Who ran and dooket in the Burn
Just at the Burnside?

But whaur are a' the old folks gane
Wha mony a year did bide?
Their dust rests in the Auld kirkyard
Quite near the Burnside.

There's naething left to mark the place
But ae hoose on Dunside
And the bonnie burnie rinnin' past
The dear auld Burnside.

E Moir, Montrose

Afterword

There is more to be discovered about Burnside of Dun, in particular from descendants of the inhabitants. If you have connections with them, or any other information about the hamlet, I would be very grateful if you could get in touch with me at

catherinemrice@yahoo.co.uk

Select Bibliography

Manuscripts, Government documents and Newspapers

Government Reports and Parliamentary Papers

Records of the Parliament of Scotland to 1707, University of St Andrews. Available online at http://www.rps.ac.uk/trans/1669/10/133. Accessed 31/1/2012.

Minutes of Evidences taken before the Poor Law Inquiry Commission for Scotland 1844, pp. 19–20. Available online from National Library of Scotland.

Reports of Assistant Handloom Weavers' Commissioners. House of Commons 27 March 1839. Irish University Press Series of British Parliamentary Papers. Industrial Revolution. Textile 9. Shannon, Ireland.

National Archives of Scotland

GD123 Papers of the Erskine Family of Dun, Angus.

CH2/1022 Records of Dun Kirk Session.

National Register of the Archives of Scotland

4346 Erskine of Dun Family Papers.

National Library of Scotland

Dep 267 Carnegy of Craigo Papers.

National Library of Scotland Map Collections

Maps of Scotland (online resource).

The British Library

BM Add. MSS 6897 The 1811 Census Enumerator.

Angus Archives

Records of the County Medical Officer of Health.

ACC 6 Angus County Council School Records.

ACC 9 Angus County Council Parochial/Parish Board Records.

MS 610 J.A. Duthie, Diary 1896–1915.

Montrose Museum

The Stool Journals, 1846–1898.

Dundee City Library
Parish of Dun Old Parish Records, 1720–1854.
Parish of Dun Census Enumerators' Books, 1841–1901.
Forfarshire Valuation Rolls, 1822–1910.

Dundee Registrars' Office
Parishes of Dun and Maryton, Registers of Births, Marriages and Deaths, 1855–1910.

Montrose Library
Montrose Standard.
Montrose Review.

Statistical Accounts of Scotland
Old Statistical Account Account of the Parish of Dun.
New Statistical Account, Account of the Parish of Dun, County of Forfar, vol.11, 1833.
3rd Statistical Account, Account of the Parish of Dun.

Books

A. Blaikie, *Illegitimacy, Sex and Society – North-East Scotland 1750–1900*, Clarendon Press, Oxford, 1993.

J. Brown and S. Ward, *The Village Shop*, Rural Development Commission, Salisbury, 1990.

M.A. Crowther, Poverty, Wealth and Welfare, in WH Fraser and RJ Morris, *People and Society in Scotland II 1830–1914*, John Donald, Edinburgh, 1990.

Allan Cunningham, *Life of Sir David Wilkie vol 1*, John Murray, London, 1843.

T.M. Devine (ed) *Farm Servants and Labour in Lowland Scotland, 1770–1914*, John Donald, Edinburgh, 1984.

J.A. Duthie, *Rhymes and Reminiscences*, D.H. Edwards, Brechin, 1912.

A. Fenton, *Scottish Country Life*, John Donald, Edinburgh, 1999.

A. Fenton and B. Walker, *The Rural Architecture of Scotland*, John Donald, Edinburgh, 1981.

M.W. Flinn (ed), *Scottish Population History from the 17th century to the 1930s*, Cambridge University Press, Cambridge, 1977.

M. Gray, Farm Workers in NE Scotland, in T. M. Devine (ed), *Farm Servants and Labour in Lowland Scotland 1770–1914*, John Donald, Edinburgh, 1984.

GUARD, *Project 795. House of Dun, Angus*, University of Glasgow, Glasgow, 2005.

A.R.B. Haldane, *The Drove Roads of Scotland*, Nelson, London, 1952.

H. Hall, *The History of Montrose Water Works*, Montrose, 1914.

J. Headrick, *General View of the Agriculture of Angus or Forfarshire*, Edinburgh, 1813.

V. Jacob, *The Lairds of Dun*, John Murray, London, 1931.

J.C. Jessop, *Education in Angus*, University of London Press, London, 1931.

W. Jolly, *The Life of John Duncan, Scotch Weaver and Botanist*, London, 1883.

J. C. Loudon, *The Manual of Cottage Gardening and Husbandry*, 1830.

F.F. Mackenzie, *Cruisie Sketches: studies of life in a Forfarshire village*, 3rd edition, Wyllie and Son, Aberdeen, 1894.

J. Morrison, *Painting the Nation*, Edinburgh University Press, Edinburgh, 2003.

N. Murray, *The Scottish Hand Loom Weavers 1790–1850: a social history*, John Donald, Edinburgh, 1978.

G. Robertson, *General View of the Agriculture of the County of Kincardine*. London, 1810.

T.C. Smout, *A Century of the Scottish People 1830–1950*, Collins, London, 1986.

J. Uglow, *A Little History of British Gardening*, Chatto and Windus, London 2004.

B. Walker, *Scottish Turf Construction. Historic Scotland Technical Advice Note 30*, Historic Scotland, Edinburgh, 2006.

B. Walker and C. McGregor *Earth Structures and Construction in Scotland. Historic Scotland Technical Advice Note 6*, Historic Scotland, Edinburgh, 1996.

C. Whatley, *Onward from Osnaburgs*, Mainstream, Edinburgh, 1992.

Articles

P. Laslett and K Oosterveen 'Long term trends in bastardy in England', *Population Studies*, Vol 27, 1973, pp 255–6.

D G Lockhart, 'Lotted lands in NE Scotland since 1850', *Journal of Scottish Historical Studies*, Vol 25, 2005 pp 119–39.

Unpublished dissertations

J. Ingram, *Geographical Mobility in Angus c. 1780–1830*. Unpublished PhD thesis, University of St Andrews, 1992.

G. Lloyd, *Linen Handloom Weavers' Houses in Scotland: a social and architectural study*, unpublished B Arch thesis, University of Dundee, 1990.

Appendices

Appendix 1a Baptisms of children born in Burnside of Dun and its predecessor settlements, 1752–1847, from the Old Parochial Registers for Dun

Surname	Christian name	Year of baptism	Surname	Christian name	Year of baptism
Mitchel	David	1752	Jemie	Margaret	1769
Prastiew?	Margaret	1752	Milne	Elizabeth	1769
Scot	Jean	1753	Thomson	David	1769
Stephen	David	1753	Young	Mary	1769
Walker	James	1753	Bertie	David	1770
Cowlie	Mary	1754	Milne	Robert	1770
Scot	Mary	1754	Thomson	James	1770
Japp	Margaret	1755	Thomson	John	1770
Stephen	Mary	1755	Jamie	Annie	1771
Webster	Isabel	1755	Milne	Jean	1771
Paterson	Isabel	1756	Young	Robert	1771
Duncan	Jean	1757	Bertie	Alexander	1773
Japp	Jean	1757	Milne	Mary	1773
Walker	William	1757	Thomson	David	1773
Webster	Anne	1757	Thomson	James	1773
Petery	James	1758	Young	Robert	1773
Stephen	James	1758	Cobb	Jean	1774
Duncan	James	1759	Gordon	Jean	1774
Mitchel	George	1759	Milne	Alexander	1774
Paterson	David	1759	Thomson	Jean	1775
Pressock	Elizabeth	1759	Thomson	Robert	1775
Walker	Elizabeth	1760	Cobb	Andrew	1776
Webster	Walter	1760	Milne	Thomas	1776
Paterson	John	1761	Hampton	Ann	1777
Barty	David	1762	Taylor	Elizabeth	1777
Belly	David	1762	Cobb	John	1778
Belly	Andrew	1763	Milne	Margaret	1778
Milne	James	1763	Thomson	Robert	1778
Berty	James	1764	Thomson	Alexander	1778
Japp	John	1764	Jamie	Alexander	1779
Paterson	Janet	1764	Petrie	James	1779
Strachan	Elizabeth	1764	Thomson	Alexander	1779
Thomson	Mary	1764	Webster	Christian	1779
Walker	David	1764	Cobb	James	1780
Young	James	1764	Cuthbert	James and William	1780
Belly	Margaret	1765			
Milne	David	1765	Thomson	Elizabeth	1780
Donn	James	1766	Nicol	William	1781
Thomson	John	1766	Petrie	Joseph	1781
			Spankie	Elizabeth	1781

Surname	Christian name	Year of baptism	Surname	Christian name	Year of baptism
Belly	Mary	1767	Mitchel	George	1799
Milne	Jean	1767	Napier	James	1801
Young	John	1767	Thomson	Isabel	1781
Bertie	Janet	1768	Duncan	James	1782
Thomson	John	1782	Milne	Helen	1782
Webster	Ann	1782	Murray	Susanna	1782
Cobb	Agnes	1783	Japp	William	1803
Duncan	John	1784	Young	James	1803
Mitchel	William	1784	Young	David	1803
Murray	James	1784	Burnett	Mary	1805
Walker	Elizabeth	1784	Gordon	John	1805
Wallace	Margaret	1784	Young	Ann	1805
Mitchel	Elizabeth	1785	Japp	James	1806
Petrie	Benjamin	1785	Gordon	Helen	1807
Thomson	Charles	1785	Robert	Susan	1807
Mitchel	John	1786	Young	John	1807
Mitchel	Nelly	1786	Young	John	1807
Murray	John	1786	Fiddes	Catherine William	1808
Mitchel	Jean	1787	Young	Elizabeth	1809
Walker	Mary	1787	Watson	Mary Ann	1810
Duncan	Robert	1788	Watson	Alice	1811
Duncan	Jean	1788	Young	George	1811
Purvis	James	1788	Fiddes	John	1812
Duncan	James	1789	Watson	John	1813
Mitchel	Agnes	1789	Watson	Elizabeth	1814
Pickyman	Alexander	1789	Rintoul	David	1815
Ritchie	John	1789	Rintoul	David	1815
Walker	Catharine	1789	Young	William	1815
Jolly	Jean	1791	Watson	Catharine	1816
Smith	William	1791	Nichol	Elizabeth	1817
Walker	Margaret and Jean	1791	Watson	Helen	1817
			Young	Janet	1817
Duncan	Margaret	1792	Nichol	Margaret	1819
Mitchel	James	1792	Smith	James	1822
Purvis	Margaret	1792	ng	Alexander Law	1823
Smith	Elizabeth	1792	Smith	William	1826
Smith	Alexander	1792	Steel	Jean	1828
Japp	Alexander	1793	Steel	James	1830
Duncan	Mary Edgar	1794	Jaffray	James	1832
Fiddes	James	1794	Steel	Margaret	1833
Smith	Catherine	1794	Jaffray	Barbara	1834
Mitchel	Euphemia	1795	Steel	Elizabeth	1836
Walker	David	1795	Young	Margaret	1836
Fiddes	Robert	1796	Young	Ann	1838
Japp	John and David	1796	Ford	Magdalene	1839
Mitchel	David	1796	Young	Jean	1839
Walker	Ann	1797	Duncan	Helen	1847

Appendix 1b List of inhabitants from Censuses, 1841–1891

Key

Ag Lab	agricultural labourer
HLW	handloom weaver

1841

Surname	Christian name	Age	Occupation	Surname	Christian name	Age	Occupation
Dour (?)	Helen	9		Mitchell	Mary	80	
Archibald	Elisabeth	45	FS	Mitchell	John	50	Linen HLW
Baillie	Jean	40	Linen HLW	Mitchell	Jean	50	
Beattie	Jean	75		Mitchell	Ann	15	Linen HLW
Brown	Francis	14	Linen HLW	Moir	David	60	Ag Lab
Christie	James	20	Linen HLW	Moir	Elizabeth	40	Linen HLW
Christie	Agnes	8		Moir	Jean	20	
Clark	Elisabeth	3		Moir	Isobel	15	female
Cruikshank	Homer	50	Grocer				servant
Cruikshank	Isobel	45		Moir	Ann	11	
Falkoner	Alexander	35	Ag Lab	Moir	Elisabeth	7	
Falkoner	Elisabeth	30		Moir	Alexander	5	
Falkoner	James	25	Wright	Moir	Jean	3	
Ford	Magdalene	40		Petrie	Ann	1	
Ford	William	30	Linen HLW	Smith	Helen	75	
Ford	Helen	9		Smith	William	70	Ag Lab
Ford	James	6		Smith	Helen	50	
Ford	Magdalene	1		Smith	Christina	45	Ag Lab
Fraser	Francis	40	Ag Lab	Smith	James	40	Linen HLW
Fraser	Margaret	35		Smith	Catherine	30	
Fraser	Ann	10		Smith	James	18	Linen HLW
Fraser	James	4		Smith	Helen	12	
Hanton (?)	Helen	75		Smith	Christina	8	
Jack	John	70	Ag Lab	Smith	Robert	75	Linen HLW
Jack	Ann	70	Ag Lab	Steel	Helen	35	
Jack	Ann	41		Steel	Alexander	30	Ag Lab
Milne	Helen	74		Steel	Joan	13	
Milne	Robert	70		Steel	Margaret	7	
Milne	Margaret	60	Independent	Steel	Elizabeth	5	
Milne	Helen	58		Steil	James	65	Ag Lab
Milne	John	25	Ag Lab	Steil	Jean	65	
Milne	Mary	24		Thomson	David	70	Farmer

Surname	Christian name	Age	Occupation
A (?)	James	28	Ag Lab
A (?)	Mary	28	HLW/Linen
A (?)	George	0.75	
Baillie	Jane	53	HLW/Linen
Bowen	John	6	Scholar at home
Brown	Francis	24	HLW/Linen
Cruikshank	Homer	58	Carrier
Cruikshank	Isabella	55	
Cunningham	Ann	43	Ag Lab
Forbe?	Isobel	7	Scholar
Forbes	Charles	25	HLW/Linen
Foreman	Elspina	58	Ag Lab
Foreman	David	45	Ag Lab
Foreman	Elizabeth	41	
Foreman	John	7	Scholar
Foreman	Elizabeth	0.5	
Gourlay	Ann	9	Scholar
Harper	James	31	Grocer and day labourer
Harper	Ann	25	Grocer and day labourer's wife
Harper	Jean D	5	Scholar
Harper	Ann	3	
Kinloch	Ann	50	
Kinloch	William	47	Linen weaver
Lawrence	Mary	35	Ag Lab
Lawrence	David	8	Scholar
Mitchell	Jean	63	Housekeeper and servant
Mitchell	John	61	HLW and teacher
Moir	Elizabeth	51	HLW/Pauper
Moir	Elizabeth	16	Housekeeper at home
Moir	Alexander	15	Scholar
Ross	Elspet	30	Shoemaker's wife
Ross	Hugh	25	Shoemaker
Smith	William	85	Ag Lab
Smith	Helen	84	
Smith	Helen	65	Pauper
Smith	Christina	54	Ag Lab
Smith	Catherine	41	Ag Lab
Smith	James	32	HLW/Linen
Smith	Helen	22	HLW/Linen
Smith	James	21	HLW/Linen
Steele	Helen	50	
Steele	Alexander	45	Day-labourer Ag Lab
Steele	Jean	28	Ag Lab

Surname	Christian name	Age	Occupation
Broadley	James	34	Ag Lab (ditcher)
Brown	Margaret	9	Scholar
Campbell	John	5	Scholar
Christie	John	3	
Cruikshank	Homer	69	Weaver (Linen)
Cruikshank	Isobella	65	
Davidson	Mary	17	Ag Lab
Duncan	William	11	
Farquhar	Margaret	71	formerly Ag lab now pauper
Ferrier	Ann	37	Housekeeper
Foreman	Elspeth	69	Ag Lab
Foreman	David	50	Ag Lab
Foreman	Elisabeth	50	
Foreman	Elisabeth	10	Scholar
Gourlay	Ann	53	Ag Lab
Harper	James	41	Ag Lab
Harper	Ann	38	
Harper	Jean D	15	
Harper	Ann	13	
Harper	William	9	Scholar
Harper	Elisabeth	7	Scholar
Harper	Isabella	3	
Heart	Peter	30	Ag Lab (ditcher)
Irons	James	8	Scholar
Jack	Alexander	59	formerly teacher now pauper
Kinloch	Ann	60	
Kinloch	Ann	60	
Kinloch	William	57	Weaver (Linen)
Kydd	Thomas	66	Ag Lab
Langoun	John	26	Ag Lab (ditcher)
Lindsay	Christina	64	formerly Ag lab
McGourty	James	30	Ag Lab (ditcher)
McHardy	Cathrine	27	
McVane	William	21	Ag Lab (ditcher)
Mill	Jane	65	
Mitchell	Helen	74	formerly domestic servant
Mitchell	Jane	73	Serv/ housekeeper
Mitchell	John	71	Weaver (Linen) and teacher of reading
Moir	Isobella	34	Weaver (Linen)
Mowat	Mary	45	Ag Lab
Pender	Thomas	34	Ag Lab (ditcher)
Pender	Thomas	6	Scholar
Pender	Mary	3	
Pender	Cathrine	1	
Ross	Jane	6	Scholar
Simond	Hellen	60	
Simpson	Ann	30	Ag Lab
Smith	James	64	Weaver (Linen)
Smith	James	38	Ag Lab
Smith	Hellen	32	Weaver (Linen)
Smith	Christina	28	Weaver (Linen)
Steel	Alexander	54	Road Lab
Steel	Isobella	17	Servant
Stoole	Elisabeth	61	Weaver (Linen)
Thomson	David	47	Grocer
Young	John	10	Scholar
Young	Elisabeth	8	Scholar

Surname	Christian name	Age	Occupation	Surname	Christian name	Age	Occupation
Brown	Margaret	19	Ag Lab	Shepherd	Jane	32	Farm Servt
Cruikshank	Homer	77	Retired weaver	Simpson	Ann	39	Ag Lab
Cruikshank	Isabell	74		Smart	Joseph	57	Ag Lab
Dalgety	John	12		Smart	Margaret K	40	
Davidson	Mary	23	Ag Lab	Smart	Joan	6	Scholar
German	James	39	Lab	Smart	Ann	3	
Gray	William	5	Scholar	Smart	Joseph	1	
McNab	James	4		Smith	James	47	Ag Lab
Morrison	Allan	37	Ag Lab	Smith	Isabella	44	
Morrison	Jane W	30		Smith	Jessie W	27	Farm Servt
Morrison	Jane	4		Smith	John	9	Scholar
Morrison	Mary	2		Smith	Jessie	7	Scholar
Morrison	Allan S	0.5		Smith	James C	3	
Mouatt	James	65	Grocer	Smith	Mary R	1	
Mouatt	Mary	62		Soutar	Elisabeth	42	
Mouatt	Helen	37	Dressmaker	Soutar	Alexander	35	Ag Lab
Mouatt	Mary W	4		Soutar	Sarah	9	Scholar
Pender	Thomas	44	Ag Lab	Soutar	Ann C	4	
Pender	Catherine	37		Steel	Helen Simm	71	
Pender	Mary	13	Servant	Steel	Alexander	66	Road Lab
Pender	Alexander	9	Scholar				
Pender	Isabella	8	Scholar	Stool	Elisabeth	71	Weaver
Pender	Jane	3		Watt	John	75	Lab
Pender	James	1		Watt	Margaret	70	
Peter	Jane	29					
Ross	Jane	16	Pauper				

1881

Surname	Christian name	Age	Occupation	Surname	Christian name	Age	Occupation
Brown	Annie	44		Pender	Catherine	47	
Burnet	Ann	59	Housekeeper	Pender	Isabella	18	Farm servant
Caird	Peter	28	Labourer general	Pender	Jane	13	Scholar
Caird	Bessie	5	Scholar	Pender	William	11	Scholar
Cruikshank	Isabella Smith	85	Retired Farm Servant	Pender	James	9	Scholar
				Pender	Henrietta	1	
				Ross	John	28	Grocer
Falconer	James	75	Retired Joiner	Ross	Isabella	24	
				Ross	Elizabeth	1	
Fyfe	Margaret	34	Farmworker	Wilkie	David	44	General labourer
Fyfe	James	15	Scholar				
Fyfe	William	12	Scholar	Wilkie	Agnes	21	General servant
Murray	Ann	48	Farm outworker	Wilkie	Alexander	15	General servant
Murray	John	13	Scholar				
Pender	Thomas	55	Farm servant	Wilkie	Annie	5	Scholar

1891

Surname	Christian name	Age	Occupation	Surname	Christian name	Age	Occupation
Davidson	Robert	73	Retired Farm Servant	Caird	Betsay	15	Servt (Farm)
				Aitkenhead	Matilda	4	
Paterson	James	35	Merchant General	Burnett	Ann	69	
				Dunmuir	George	71	Farm labourer
Paterson	Ann	32					
Paterson	James	10	Scholar	Dunmuir	Ann	75	
Paterson	Alexander	7	Scholar	Milne	Elizabeth	55	Cook
Paterson	William	5	Scholar	Milne	David	16	Farm servant
Connor	Peter	60	Ag Lab				
Connor	Ann	60		Milne	Maggie	13	Scholar
Caird	Peter	38	Ag Lab	Milne	Jane	9	Scholar

Index

Strachan, Barbara 42
Strachan, David 69
Strathdon 22,
Simond or Symm, Helen 29, 31

Taranty Tryst 5,13, 22, 89
Tayock 38, 44, 87
Thomson, David 16, 27
Thomson, John 27
Thomson, John (mapmaker) 6, 15
tileworks (at Mains of Dun) 31, 32, 55, 67
Trinity Fair see Taranty Tryst
turf (for building) 7, 55, 57
turnips 7, 32

Walker, William 16, 57
Wallace, James 31
Watt, John and Margaret 62, 82
wells 19, 90
West Leys of Dun see Leys of Dun
Wilkie family 30
wright 16, 19, 25, 68

Young, John 44
Young, Elizabeth 44, 79
Young, James 44
Young, John, smith 15, 27, 69

The Abertay Historical Society

The Society was founded in May 1947 and exists to promote interest in local history. For membership forms and further information, please visit our website at **www.abertay.org.uk**

Publications of the Abertay Historical Society currently in print

No.37   Michael St John, *The Demands of the People, Dundee Radicalism*
         1850-1870. (1997)
         ISBN 978 0 900019 33 3

No.39   Lorraine Walsh, *Patrons, Poverty & Profit: Organised Charity in*
         Nineteenth Century Dundee. (2000)
         ISBN 978 0 900019 35 7

No.41   Ian McCraw, *Victorian Dundee at Worship.* (2002)
         ISBN 978 0 900019 37 9

No.42   Andrew Murray Scott, *Dundee's Literary Lives vol 1: Fifteenth*
         to Nineteenth Century. (2003)
         ISBN 978 0 900019 38 7

No 43   Andrew Murray Scott, *Dundee's Literary Lives vol 2:*
         Twentieth Century. (2004)
         ISBN 978 0 900019 39 5

No 45   Annette M. Smith, *The Guildry of Dundee: A History of the*
         Merchant Guild of Dundee up to the 19th century. (2005)
         ISBN 978 0 900019 42 5

No 46   Mary Verschuur, *A Noble and Potent Lady: Katherine Campbell,*
         Countess of Crawford. (2006)
         ISBN 978 0 900019 43 2

No 47   Kenneth Cameron, *The Schoolmaster Engineer: Adam Anderson of Perth*
         & St Andrews 1780-1846. (2007)
         ISBN 978 0 900019 44 9

No 48   Sarah F. Browne, *Making the Vote Count: The Arbroath*
         Womens' Citizens Association, 1931-1945. (2007)
         ISBN 978 0 900019 45 6

No 49   Ann Petrie, *The 1915 Rent Strikes: An East Coast Perspective.* (2008)
         ISBN 978 0 900019 46 3

No 51   Matthew Jarron *et al* (editors), *Ten Taysiders: Forgotten Figures from Dundee, Angus and Perthshire.* (2011)
ISBN 978 0 900019 48 7

No 52   Susan Keracher, *Dundee's Two Intrepid Ladies: A Tour Round the World by D.C. Thomson's Female Journalists in 1894.* (2012)
ISBN 978 0 900019 49 4

No 54   Julie S Danskin, *A City at War: The 4th Black Watch, Dundee's Own.* (2013)
ISBN 978 0 900019 51 7

All publications may be obtained through booksellers or by post from the Hon Sales Secretary, Abertay Historical Society, Alder Archaeology, 55 South Methven Street, Perth, PH1 5NX (e-mail: csmith@alderarchaeology.co.uk)